Praise for
The Mastectomy I Always Wanted

"A must-read for anyone facing the diagnosis of breast cancer. Erica writes about her lived experience with a vulnerability and ease that will surround you with hope and support. And, importantly, she gives simple and empowering actions that you can take from the start to end of your journey."

—**Tia Newcomer**, CEO of CaringBridge

"*The Mastectomy I Always Wanted* is an honest and vulnerable story about a cancer diagnosis and subsequent mastectomy. It is a good guide for women who hear those words, 'You have breast cancer.' The real-life photos are used with purpose. They show a true level of the pain but end with the freedom of recovery and reconstruction."

—**Christine Handy**, breast cancer survivor, international speaker, accomplished model, best-selling author, and a nationally recognized humanitarian

"The pictures: courageous, powerful, beautiful. Made me know everything will be okay for my wife."

—**Adam Shiffman**, husband to breast cancer and mastectomy survivor

"This book is a must-read for anyone who has experienced breast cancer or is a caregiver to someone impacted by cancer. Erica shares her own journey with cancer using an authentic voice, while also showing the vast amount of emotions that this disease brings from the time of diagnosis to surgery. Real, raw, and beautifully written to capture what cancer survivors experience in the whirlwind that is a cancer diagnosis."

—**Amy Gallagher**, executive director of the Firefly Sisterhood and BRCA1+ previvor

"This book is inspiring, raw, and authentic—and deeply needed in the conversation about breast cancer for women and caregivers."

—**Holly Tyson**, board member for the Cancer Support Community

THE MASTECTOMY I ALWAYS WANTED

A Breast Cancer Memoir

ERICA NEUBERT CAMPBELL

Wise Ink
—Minneapolis, MN—

The Mastectomy I Always Wanted © copyright 2024 by Erica Neubert Campbell. All rights reserved. No part of this book may be reproduced in any form whatsoever, by photography or xerography or by any other means, by broadcast or transmission, by translation into any kind of language, nor by recording electronically or otherwise, without permission in writing from the author, except by a reviewer, who may quote brief passages in critical articles or reviews.

ISBN 13: 978-1-63489-709-9
Library of Congress Catalog Number has been applied for.
Printed in the United States of America
First Printing: 2024
28 27 26 25 24   5 4 3 2 1

Cover design by Emily Mahon
Interior design by Vivian Steckline
Interior photography by Erica Neubert Campbell
Author photo by *Minneapolis/St. Paul Business Journal*
Editing by Sara Letourneau
Proofreading by Zenyse Miller and Elizabeth Farry
Production editor: Dara Beevas

Wise Ink
PO Box 580195
Minneapolis, MN 55458-0195

Wise Ink is a creative publishing agency for game-changers. Wise Ink authors uplift, inspire, and inform, and their titles support building a better and more equitable world. For more information, visit WiseInk.com.

To order, visit ItascaBooks.com or www.EricaNeubertCampbell.com. Reseller discounts available.

Contact Erica Neubert Campbell at www.EricaNeubertCampbell.com for speaking engagements, freelance writing projects, and interviews.

To my mother, a humble leader and powerful guardian angel.

To you, for opening this book and letting me walk beside you.

Someone I loved once gave me
a box full of darkness.

It took me years to understand
that this, too, was a gift.

— Mary Oliver, "The Uses of Sorrow"

Author's Note

I have an influential mentor who refuses to give me advice. Instead, he shares a story about his experience, and I listen. He doesn't assume he has all the answers. I'm given the opportunity to take what works given my own challenging situation. As a result, I learn to decide with confidence and trust myself.

This is my intention. I am sharing my personal experience for you to take what you need. I understand you are managing fears about cancer, breasts, femininity, health, and even death. I faced these things, too. However, I do not know the details of your circumstances. Your journey is highly personal. I hope there are nuggets here to inspire your choices, deepen your reflection, and strengthen your inner voice. You already have everything you need.

I'm not a doctor. I don't pretend to have all the answers. However, I am a woman who powerfully chose to move forward with a mastectomy and found success. My experience is that my breasts are even better than before. More importantly, my fears of relapse or cancer spreading are gone. This is what I want for you. If you are deciding between avoiding surgery, electing a lumpectomy, or choosing a mastectomy, I encourage the mastectomy. Feel free to debate this. Feel free to tell me that women's bodies should not be altered. Feel free to be afraid or angry. My only request is to be yourself.

I'm here to vulnerably and intimately share my experience and tell you it will be okay.

Introduction: This Is for You

When I was first diagnosed, a woman from work, we'll call her Sophia, heard about my upcoming mastectomy. After a team meeting, she pulled me aside. "I had a double mastectomy and reconstructive surgery about five years ago," she whispered.

I was speechless. Her body looked healthy and beautiful. Plus, I barely knew her.

"I'm afraid," I said quietly. "I don't know what to expect."

"You are going to be fine," she said with knowing eyes and confidence. "Trust me."

"Will I ever be the same again?" I asked.

She paused and smiled with deep kindness.

"Are you okay with seeing my breasts?" she replied.

I was deeply interested in knowing my future yet desperately trying to stay professional. Curiosity and courage won.

We found a bathroom off the beaten path in the office and locked the door for privacy. Then Sophia showed me her breasts with no hesitation. My heart jumped in surprise, and my eyes widened. Her reconstructed, fake breasts looked so natural that I did not believe she'd had a mastectomy with her nipples removed. She had scars so faint that I had to squint to see them and 3D nipple tattoos that looked like genuine body parts. Out of disbelief, I awkwardly asked to touch them. The eyes can deceive, and my heart wanted to believe.

Sophia gave me hope. The authentic connection and support made me believe this was not the end. I could see the future as I stood behind the starting line. I am forever grateful to Sophia for being courageous in sharing her story and generously revealing this part of herself. She started a domino effect of acceptance and resilience for me. I received concrete advice and candid humor. Because of her vulnerability, I could see my future, which looked happy, healthy, and healed.

This book is intended to be a similar experience. Imagine you and I are standing together in an office bathroom as new friends. I want you to have an intimate view of the mastectomy journey, which includes a validation of the fears, questions, and mental obstacles. Let's shine a light on the authentic emotions and the physical journey, no matter how personal or awkward it may be. I hope you gain hope, validate your feelings, and build resilience. I want you to find comfort in knowing that you will be okay. Lock the door behind you and read on.

This is for you.

ONE

STRANGE BEGINNINGS

Hardships often prepare ordinary people for an extraordinary destiny.

— C. S. Lewis

The Waiting

Waiting for test results is the worst. Even though I stayed busy during the workday, my mind wandered into worst-case scenarios. The possibility of cancer clouded the ability to be fully present after several days with no phone call about the test results. My left breast was still sore and bruised from a biopsy performed earlier in the week. The agony of not knowing grew. I regularly checked my cell phone to ensure the ringer volume was up. Anxiety gnawed at me, making me wonder if the doctor's office had misplaced my results or forgotten about me.

I jumped when my cell phone finally rang at 4:12 p.m. I raced out of a meeting without saying goodbye and quickly closed the door to my office.

The nurse on the phone asked me to sit down. She explained that the biopsy had revealed several malignancies, and she diagnosed me with early-stage breast cancer called ductal carcinoma in situ (DCIS). I did not know what she was saying. All I heard was "breast cancer." My world shifted and I lost focus. I stared at the jumble of words I scribbled on scrap paper, wondering how to tell my husband and kids. I assumed I was going to die.

This was not the first time I'd heard the phrase "breast cancer." My mother died from a long, arduous battle with the disease fifteen years ago. I walked nearly every step of the journey with her. Unfortunately, she relapsed four times before cancer took her life. Witnessing how cancer slowly consumed her body and soul scarred me forever.

Now, here I was at age forty-five, facing a similar diagnosis. I feared this moment for years. I always suspected breast cancer was in my future.

Up until now, no one listened. I spent most of my thirties meeting with gynecologists, breast specialists, and genetic counselors who told me not to worry. Even though I tested negative for the BRCA gene, the continuous cycle of fear swirled within me. I often got called back after mammograms for further testing to look closely at suspicious spots and breast calcifications. The extra caution caused "scanxiety" every few months and wore me down.

In 2013, the famous actress Angelina Jolie wrote a vulnerable and authentic article in the *New York Times* about the double mastectomy she chose after genetic tests revealed her increased risk of breast cancer. Her vulnerability inspired many women to take control of their bodies and get a preventative mastectomy, ultimately saving more lives. Soon after, the rise in these prophylactic mastectomies was called "The Angelina Jolie Effect." Because my cancer fears often overtook me, I wanted to get a preventative mastectomy to reduce my risk and remove continuous worry. Over the years, several doctors smiled politely and scoffed at my request. They said that even though my mom died of breast cancer, my level of risk was the same as the general population. I logically understood the statistics, but I still believed breast cancer was in my future.

I didn't want to be too self-righteous, but now I was facing the diagnosis.

I predicted this moment.

I was finally right.

The problem was the memory of my mom's breast cancer journey. Her cancer started small, and she treated it lightly. She chose a lumpectomy to remove only the pea-sized cancerous spots in her breast and trusted that was enough. But it was not. She relapsed four times in four years, and I sat in several meetings with doctors who shook their heads in surprise at how her breast cancer spread.

A few months before she died, I sat with her in the hospital for complications from her treatment. Her regular physician was out of town for the holidays, and we met with a new, young doctor covering the late-night shift. He scanned her thick medical file and wondered out loud.

"I'm surprised your mom only had a lumpectomy in the beginning. She might not have relapsed if she chose a mastectomy instead," he said. This comment burned in my soul.

The aggressive nature of her cancer eventually took her life. The disease spread to her bones, lungs, and brain, and I witnessed a slow and painful death. On the day she took her final breath, I gently stroked her right hand and encouraged her to let go. My beliefs about compassion and trust were shattered, and her death forever changed me.

In the years after she died, I struggled with guilt and questions. If she had opted for a mastectomy rather than a lumpectomy at the start of her treatment plan, I believed she would still be alive today. I wished I had been more informed about her surgical choices. Although I understood the emotional risks of looking in the rearview mirror of medical decisions, my heart tore open. This regret haunted me. I wished I could turn back time and longed for a different ending.

Before I was diagnosed, I swore this would not be me someday. I told myself I would choose differently. Now here I was, the main character in my breast cancer story. The magnitude of fear and self-doubt already started with the word *cancer*. I buckled in for the roller coaster of emotions and experiences ahead. My world began to shift like an earthquake splitting open the ground, and I decided to choose where to stand.

At first, the options presented to me seemed endless. Like my mom, the surgical choices were a lumpectomy to remove only the cancerous breast tissue or a mastectomy to remove the whole breast. A lumpectomy would come with possible radiation, hormone therapy, and even chemotherapy. A single mastectomy would remove cancer in the left breast but leave the fear of cancer in the right breast someday. A double mastectomy would remove both breasts and the fear of cancer. I remembered my mother's journey. I knew what to do.

This was the double mastectomy I always wanted.

TWO

DIAGNOSIS TO SURGERY: POETRY TO ME

I write entirely to find out what I'm thinking, what I'm looking at, what I see and what it means. What I want and what I fear.

—Joan Didion

Tears and Fears

I've been crying a little
a lot of the time,
which feels great.
Overdue, in fact.

Like the tipping of a giant vat of tears,
letting out enough to stay stable,
not swaying too hard
in one direction
to destabilize and cause a flood.

Not watershed tears,
just the release valve of a pressure cooker.
The crying feels like
it will heal other wounds
that have never closed
or been washed clean.

Grief is so dirty.
It's dust under the feet of death and loss.
In the past, I didn't cry or talk
as much as I should have.

I am stronger than I think.
This is silly.
I'm healthy.

I need less booze and stress,
and more veggies.
There are fears,
and then there are FEARS.
I know waiting is the worst.

A Letter from My MRI

Here's a letter from my MRI:

Bring earphones.
Bring an eye mask.
Bring the piano music you listened to
while birthing your children.
This is only a test.
It's going to be okay.

My reply:
The only thing
I will bring
is me.

I already have
everything
I need.

Too Many Choices

The words from doctors come at me
like water from a firehose.
Fierce and fast.
I'm drowning in words I don't understand.
Receptors, margins, nodes, probability, genetics.
Words. Tests. Results.
How bad is it?
Is there a good cancer?

Deciding what to do next
Is like choosing a deadly weapon
When I didn't pick the battle.
I want to fight, but not like this.
I must make a choice.

Debating is such a time suck.
And it's so embarrassing.
How can I trust myself
when my body is not listening?
I wish someone else would decide.
I need clarity.
Or fewer doctor appointments.
The choices I have to make are hard.
The choices I get to make are harder.

For Now

It's going to be okay!
This is what the MRI told me.
My cancer has not spread.
For now, at least.
I feel a huge weight lift from
my chest, shoulders—and boobs.
Now we know the size of the beast.
Fear is still a shadow chasing me.
I'll stay so busy
I won't think about it.
For now.

Communications

Communications are hard.
Who to tell, who not to tell.
How to respond to texts,
Who, what, when, where
It's all so complex and demanding.

I can't take care of others and their emotions.
Questions come from curiosity and distress.
They want to learn what I'm going through
in case it happens to them.

What people want to hear:
Details and hope.

What I want to say:
Cancer is not contagious.

Unsexy

I'm sitting across the table,
looking at black-and-white photos of my breasts.
Learning about density, false positives,
and calcifications.

It's exhausting to look at my breasts this way.
I try to be objective and factual, like the doctor.
I am so done.

You'd think my husband and I
would be sending each other
sexy pictures of my breasts.
No—just black, white, and gray ones,
with speckled spider attributes.
Clinical and careful.

No fifty shades of gray here.
No beauty.
I am so *done*.

Daily Journey

Telling people sucks.
I do it at random,
and the different reactions are interesting:
from sympathy to humor.
I prefer laughter,
but pity can't help itself.
It creeps in.
If I softly chuckle with a friend about getting new boobs,
pity poisons the conversation.

Some people said they were sorry.
Sorry for what?
Some people said I was brave.
Brave about what?
Some people sent ribbons.
It's too late for pink.

Many people revealed their fears about cancer.
I wanted to shout
It's not about you.
My dad freaked out.
I found myself consoling him.

One dude asked me if I blamed God.
I blamed him for asking that terrible question.

The Mastectomy I Always Wanted

Some people asked too many questions.
Some people needed to ask more.
Some people were helpful.
Some were not.

The Ferris wheel of telling the news to people
Kept going in circles.
It was a daily journey to the circus.
Some sweets and a few clowns.

FATE

I've decided to choose this mastectomy.
It's possible my fate was decided a long time ago.
Did I bargain with God and lose the bet?

Thy will be done.
A prayer I've recited a million times.
I wondered if I brought this upon myself.
Did I accidentally ask for this?
I take it back.

There is nothing to beat
but my fears.
My fate feels out of control.
My fear is that I am.

Regret is not worth the effort.
Because really, I will overcome.
It's the double mastectomy
I always wanted.

Self-Pity

Welcome to self-pity, party of one.
While I sit here by myself,
I invite a few bitter guests to the table.
How fun!
Let's meet them.

I'm not a good mom.
I'm jealous of other women who eat healthy
and seem to have it all (but they don't, right?).
I brought on this bad luck (which is probably good luck in disguise, right?).
I can't get my kids to bed on time.
I have too much clutter.
I want an easier life.
I'm so tired of my sad stories.
They're old and boring.

Too much expectation.
Too little time.
I'm too stubborn.
I'm not stubborn enough.
I feel so alone at this pity party.
I might break.
It's not *pretty*.
I need to be selfish
even though I already think I am.

Three Truths

I realized these truths:

1. I have good instincts.

2. Struggling is okay.

3. Many people love me.

Dang.

This means:

4. Cancer requires trust.

5. Cancer is a connector.

6. Cancer is a bitch.

Why Me?

Why me?
Of course, it's me.

I created a story.
Cancer wasn't a matter of if, but when.
No one believed me,
except me.

I asked for a preventative mastectomy
and was shot down.

They told me,
You're not at risk.
It's not needed.
Fuck you.

I was right.
Again!

This is proof
that life is not fair.
No one plans for cancer.
And I will never give up.

Turn the World Upside Down

I am,
wild,
determined,
visionary,
and I never give up.
Years ago, I witnessed someone
Lift off into a handstand at the gym,
Graceful, strong, free.
Impossible,
I thought.

And a seed was planted.
I studied and failed for three years.
I wobbled, tumbled, and fell,
Until I developed my own grace and strength.

One week before this surgery
My vision came to life
I turned the world upside down
And achieved a handstand.
Three years of work
for three seconds in the air.

When I love myself,
I move mountains.

The Mastectomy I Always Wanted

I can do it again.
As Harriet Beecher Stowe said,
Never give up,
for that is just the time and place
the tide will turn.
I will be like Harriet.

Bring it on, surgery.

Fast-Forward

I want to fast-forward
to the healing place,
but
I must walk through
the tunnel of pain and fear
to get there.

Wait,
walk,
worry.

I want to run.
Lord,
please help me
be at peace
and rest.

This, too, shall pass.
I tell myself
I am fearless and fierce.

Never Give Up

Tomorrow is a new day.
I need to stress less.
There is so much to do,
but God laughed at my plans.

The daily chores,
the big projects,
the annual goals.

Good try!
He whispered.
These tasks will subside.

Let it go.
Give in and surrender—
but don't give up!

Stop Worrying

Ugh.
I hate worrying,
because it reminds me
that I'm upset.
I want to sleep.
I want life to be easier.
I want, I want, I want.
I worry,
I worry,
I worry.

A voice rises.

It will be easier.
Be kind to yourself.
Prioritize what matters.
You
will
get
through
this.
Have faith in the journey
Stop worrying.

THREE

WHAT WE TOLD PEOPLE

Never assume a person who has difficulty communicating has nothing to say.

— Stacy Sekinger

I Hate Telling You This in an Email . . .

Dearest friends and family,

There is no other way to say this. I was recently diagnosed with early-stage breast cancer in my left breast, which was caught very early through a routine mammogram. It's called ductal carcinoma in situ, or DCIS, and it's considered Stage 0 on a scale of 1 to 4 (so that's good!).

Given my family history, I will treat it aggressively and have a double mastectomy with breast reconstructive surgery on Wednesday, May 16. It will be a challenging surgery, but I'm at peace with it. I will recover stronger—and with some new boobs!

I'm trying to focus on the positive and laugh where possible. It's going to be okay.

We will inform people of progress via email. In addition, my friend Lynne has helpfully prepared detailed instructions below on how to help and FAQs below about what I'm facing.

Honestly, saying these words is hard. I would have preferred to tell each of you over a carefully made cappuccino or a delightfully cool glass of sauvignon blanc. I want to call and respond to everyone, but I can't.

Your love and support are important to me, but please don't feel bad if I don't answer the phone or respond to your message. Communicating about this is a bit overwhelming, so please send questions or notes to my husband, Ian.

This is a "bump in the road"—and this could be the best thing that ever happened to me. I can't get breast cancer in the future because I won't have breasts. (Don't worry, I'll get fake ones soon.)

I've got a ton of support, and I'm deeply grateful. Ian and I will keep you posted.

It's going to be okay—I pinky swear promise!

Lots of love,

Erica (and Ian) XO

PS: This is not a secret, so feel free to share it with others as you wish. I may have missed a few people!

Erica Health FAQs

1. What can I do to help?

Send Erica positive text messages or cards to let her know you are thinking about her.

A. If you are local and want to make a meal, sign up on Meal Train.

B. Send Erica an Instacart gift certificate. Instacart is a delivery service allowing her to purchase items from many stores, including Whole Foods, Fresh Thyme Farmers Market, Costco, CVS, and Total Wine & More. Please buy any gift cards under Ian's email address.

C. If you live nearby, any help with babysitting and entertaining her children Amelia and Duncan is helpful.

D. Do NOT send flowers. If you want to send something, Erica is in the market for inspirational quotes to put on the wall in her home or office. Feel free to send any pictures, plaques, or signs, and we'll get them on the wall.

E. Erica will have a lot of time at home after the surgery. Any suggestions on how to stay occupied are welcome (e.g., TV series or movies you'd recommend).

2. How can I find out how Erica's surgery went?

Ian will send a group update once the surgery is complete.

3. Anything I should avoid?

Erica will be managing a lot during this time. The amount of support from her friends and family is so kind and appreciated. It will be hard for Erica to respond to each message she receives, so it would be appreciated if your correspondence focused on words of encouragement rather than questions for her to answer.

4. What kind of cancer does Erica have?

Erica has Stage 0, noninvasive ductal carcinoma in situ (DCIS), meaning that abnormal cells have been found in the lining of the milk ducts in her left breast. Generally, treatment options include a lumpectomy with radiation or a mastectomy. However, Erica is planning a radical double mastectomy since her mom died of breast cancer.

5. What is Erica's prognosis?

Because DCIS is noninvasive, Erica's chances of recovery and long-term survival are extremely high. She has many more years ahead of leadership in her Pinky Swear Foundation work, plus other fun things like teaching dance classes; wearing glitter and leopard print; being an amazing mom, wife, daughter, and sister; and making us laugh and smile.

6. Is this the same type of cancer Erica's mom had?

No. Erica's mom had a different type of breast cancer that was further along when diagnosed.

7. How did Erica find out?
Erica found out as the result of a standard mammogram and a subsequent biopsy.

8. What additional testing has Erica done since the initial diagnosis?
Erica had an MRI done to determine if there was any additional cancer. None was found. This includes no cancer identified in her lymph nodes.

9. What type of treatment has Erica decided on?
Erica is moving forward with a double mastectomy scheduled for Wednesday, May 16. This treatment will give her the best chance at avoiding any future cancer diagnosis. She will get breast reconstruction performed over a three-to-six-month period. After the May 16 surgery, she will start with expanders to help stretch out her skin a little at a time. These will be placed under her chest muscles. She will then get the final breast augmentation surgery done at the end of that period.

10. Where will Erica's surgery be performed? And how long will she be at the hospital?
Methodist Hospital in St. Louis Park. She will be in the hospital for one night, two at most.

11. Who will be with Erica during her surgery?
Ian will be with Erica during her surgery. Local family

members will help watch the kids, and her dad will visit soon, too.

12. Will Erica need to do chemo or radiation?
This depends on the results of the tissue testing once Erica's double mastectomy is complete. Thus far, the doctors do not believe she will need either.

13. How long will Erica's recovery be?
Erica will be out of work for two to four weeks following the surgery. Her body will continue to recover for some time after that. She might be unable to do strenuous exercise involving her upper body for nine months. However, she can do lots of walking and lower body exercises after her initial recovery.

14. How is Erica feeling?
Erica is understandably anxious about the diagnosis and the upcoming surgery. However, her outlook and attitude are positive. She is a fighter and a doer, and she looks forward to kicking this cancer in the butt!

15. Wait—I have more questions! Who should I ask?
Email her husband, Ian Campbell, and we'll add it to these FAQs.

Why Not Me?

Someone recently asked me,
Are you struggling with the "Why me?" question?
(PS: That's a mildly unhelpful question.)
But the answer is truly no.
(Even after reflecting on the question
and a gut check.)

I reconciled that question years ago
when my mother—
a healthy, faithful,
no-chance-of-recurrence woman—
got the news
that her cancer had returned.
Again.

But that is *not* me.
I do not intend to let this cancer spread.
Her recurrences shattered the most inherent promise
I made with God and fate.

Bad things happen to good people.
Life is not fair.
It has never been fair
for people who are or have been
persecuted or left behind,
sick or disabled.

I am in between
With plenty of room for deep,
dark spots of gray fear.

T-Minus Two Days

Do you have the best doctors?
I don't know.
Did you choose the right course of action?
I don't know.
You should get a second opinion.
Doesn't mine count?

Everyone asks me what I want,
Then tells me what to do.

Who gives a fuck
about others' opinions?
Focus on the good.
It's all good!

I'm so tired.
Be still
And listen to the inner voice
That says you are good enough.

I will get through this.
Forget the fears.
They shall not be named.
If they have names,
They have power.

I want more time with my children.
They are my growth path.
My reasons to not miss my life.

FOUR

PRIVATE GOODBYES

How lucky am I to have something that makes saying goodbye so hard.

— A. A. Milne

The End of the Beginning

I went to my beloved noontime yoga class the day before my surgery. As I progressed through each move, I began to cry. I intensely noticed how much I used my chest and shoulders for stretches, cobra positions, and handstands. With heightened awareness, I felt the sting of sadness and anticipatory grief. Yoga was no longer in my future.

I made so much progress over the last three years. I finally felt powerful and confident in complex poses. I could do a backbend, hold myself up in a crow position, and upside down in a headstand. My doctor had told me I would get this all back eventually, but I did not believe him. I would have no breasts for a sports bra, let alone the strength to hold my body weight.

After class, I sheepishly asked the instructor to photograph me in these poses. My eyes welled again as I shared the news of my upcoming double mastectomy, which would end my yoga practice. The high of this yoga class was like partying on the last day before college graduation. I believed my glory days were ending.

She tilted her head at me in curiosity.

"Maybe your yoga journey is starting," she said.

I did not understand.

"Come back to class," she said, straightening up to hold my phone. "Just sit and breathe."

The Mastectomy I Always Wanted

Me, Myself, and I

I went home from yoga class confused. How could my yoga journey be starting after years of work? I suspected my yoga efforts could be on pause, but "just beginning" didn't make sense.

I began to accept the impending loss of my breasts even though they played a big part in my life. As a teenager, I started as a late bloomer who desperately wanted to grow breasts. My friends at sixteen confidently showed their cleavage in tight tops while I hid my bare chest in baggy shirts. I often leaned over in the mirror to see if gravity would make my breasts pop out sooner. My self-worth tied into my appearance, and I blamed a lack of high school boyfriends on a flat chest. By the time I graduated college, a combination of time and "the freshman fifteen" resulted in glorious breasts that finally made me proud. Then, over the next twenty years, my magnificent breasts excelled in their job. They drew attention at house parties or bars during my dating years. Once I finally found my soul mate, my cleavage looked fabulous in a wedding dress. When my children were born, these breasts provided milk and nutrients to help them grow. Miracles happened because of my breasts.

Sadly, these breasts also caused years of anxiety and sorrow. I endured regular "fear fests" in the form of mammograms and conversations with doctors I didn't understand. Weeks before and after a mammogram came, my stomach ached from the anxiety associated with the underlying possibility of breast cancer. Every round of tests brought back memories of my mom's journey and left one more doubt in the back of my mind. These fears stayed with me like a heavy backpack I carried, weighing me down without knowing.

On the day before my mastectomy, I stood topless in front of my bedroom mirror and held my breasts in my hands. The time to say goodbye was upon me. The mere thought of such extensive surgery and extreme discomfort was terrifying. I began to realize that the loss of my breasts meant more than the loss of flesh or nipples. But the fear of dying from breast cancer loomed larger. I had to choose which was more difficult—the memory of the past or the anxiety of the future. These breasts would no longer serve me. I had to let them go, and I didn't want to forget.

I remembered a concept from one of my favorite authors, Joan Didion, about life experiences. She mused that beginnings were clear, but endings were harder to see. I wanted to create this ending and remember it.

I recalled advice from my work friend, Sophia, and bravely committed to documenting my body on this day before the mastectomy. This was my private celebration of me. I created a "going away" party of one, consisting of selfies of my bare breasts and my proudest yoga poses. These were the breasts I had wanted since I was thirteen years old. I thanked them for their service. They had done their job. I celebrated the growth, the transformation, the confidence, the struggles, the life-giving milk for babies—and the end of the journey. This mastectomy was my choice. I was choosing myself, no matter the pain and changes to my body. I was choosing to end the fear of cancer and begin the journey to freedom. Once again, this was the mastectomy I always wanted.

The Mastectomy I Always Wanted

The Night Before Surgery

In our house,
the two most common phrases
my children hear are
"No problem!"
and "Never give up."

The advice we give our children
is a mirror onto ourselves.

This will be no problem
because I will never give up.
Take that, cancer.
Take that, life.

See you on the other side.

  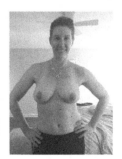

Stepping Off the Treadmill of Life

On the morning of my surgery, I sat at the kitchen counter with no makeup and old clothes. I had already been fasting for the last eight hours. I left my wedding rings tucked away in my underwear drawer as instructed. Without water or my beloved morning coffee, I already began to feel disoriented. When it was finally time to go, I said quick goodbyes to my children, hiding the heaviness in my heart. I didn't want to scare them, or more importantly, I didn't want to add further to my anxiety. I had already thrown out all my bras.

As we drove in morning traffic, I felt the world buzzing with to-dos and places to be. The sky was crystal blue, and the air had a crisp anticipation of spring. Yet I could not appreciate the beginning of this new season. I felt cheated out of the summer ahead. My busy life was pausing, forced to step off the treadmill of life for a while. My husband and I solemnly pulled into the concrete parking deck, holding hands as soon as we locked the car.

The silent walk from the parking lot to the surgery check-in line felt like an anticipated death march. I slowly transitioned to solemn reflection. My feet moved deliberately, fighting the desire to run back to the car. I had dreaded this day for weeks. Yet, there was relief in knowing the waiting was over. The journey to this moment had been like running through mud, even as I tried not to resist it.

I stood in line behind other people checking in for surgery at the administrative desk and attempted to guess their ailments. These strangers did not know the surgery I was facing. I overheard small talk of shoulder surgeries and ingrown toenails. No one looked afraid or concerned. When it was my turn to register, the clerk seemed unfazed when I told her I was there for a mastectomy. She did not show pity but rather a look of boredom. I mildly appreciated her nonchalant attitude to her job. My paperwork was her daily treadmill of life; I was on mine.

She pointed left to go upstairs to the pre-surgical registration desk by myself. Separating from my husband was symbolic and painful. I walked the long hallway corridor alone and stepped onto the elevator. A deep sense of loneliness exploded inside me.

Even though he and I would reunite before the surgery, I deeply felt a separation. I was taking the next big step on my own. The only person who could do this was me.

I Got This

Behind a thin curtain, I removed all my clothes and put my belongings in a plastic bag. My life boiled down to a driver's license, a cell phone, and lip balm. Everything was stripped away from me, with nothing left to hide.

Cheerful and kind nurses arrived in rapid succession. I laid on an incline table wrapped in a thin paper gown and uncomfortable socks. To keep me warm, one nurse offered me extra blankets and attached an air hose to my paper gown that pumped in warm air. My outfit blew up like an inflatable mattress around me. I looked bigger but felt small.

The magnitude and anxiety continued through the small decisions I got to make as I waited. One nursing assistant offered lavender essential oil to calm my nerves. I accepted, even though I wasn't convinced a relaxing scent would make a difference. The anesthesiologist asked if I preferred my left or right arm for the needles needed for surgery. I worried my veins would collapse as much as my hope. Deep down, I wanted my husband and care team to think I was confident. The inner voices in my head shouted obscenities and terror, but I looked calm on the outside.

While I waited for the final pre-visit from the surgeon, the anesthesiologist offered the option of a cocktail of relaxation drugs to be injected into my saline drip to take off the edge. I immediately accepted, and relief began to course through my veins. I drifted into a boozy state as if I had chugged three glasses of wine.

Once those anxious voices fell silent, I could hear the other voice growing in my head—the gentle voice that had been crowded out by fear:

I got this.

I got this.

I got this.

FIVE

WHAT I DON'T REMEMBER

*It's not what you say to everyone else that determines your life;
it's what you whisper to yourself that has the greatest power.*

— Robert T. Kiyosaki

The Day of the Surgery

May 16

Hi all,

Just wanted to send a quick update on Erica. Bottom line: things went as well as we could have hoped.

Both the general surgeon and the plastic surgeon reported that their respective procedures went well. Most importantly, they did a lymph node biopsy, and the real-time result was negative (meaning no cancer in the lymph nodes!). They will do a full pathology report, so we won't know for another two to three days, but this is the best outcome we could have hoped for.

Erica is trying to get some rest in the hospital room—she was in the OR for six hours and is in a lot of pain. We'll be here at the hospital for at least one night. You will not be surprised that she has shown incredible grit, determination, and strength today. As she was rolled out of her pre-op room this morning, the relaxation drugs were definitely taking effect, but she grabbed my arm and said, "Tell everyone I got this." Indeed, she's got this.

Then this evening, when I could finally see her in the

hospital room minutes after she left the post-anesthesia care unit, the nurses and I told her she did a great job—and with eyes closed, she mumbled, "Because I'm a badass." Indeed, she's that.

Thank you, everyone, for your prayers, messages of encouragement, positive vibes, and whatever else you did leading up to today. They clearly worked.

This is one step in a longer journey, and we'll let you know how things progress. Immediate next steps are pain management, post-op stabilization, and rest.

We'll keep everyone posted. Again, apologies in advance if we're slow to respond. Keep sending messages to me.

Hugs,

Ian (and Erica)

SIX

GROUND ZERO: DAZED AND CONFUSED

It is cruel irony: Most times our greatest strengths are birthed from our darkest days.

— Natalie Jensen

The Itch

I woke up.

I did not fully remember
where I was
and what I was there for.

I did not want
to move.

I just wanted
to stay still
and feel.

My throat hurt.

My lips were dry.

My legs were being squeezed
by something like the floaties
that kids wear on their arms
when they are learning how to swim.

I wanted water.

My husband

and a nurse
were standing above me.

My mind sharpened
as they spoke.

My body was cocooned
by pillows.

I looked down at my chest
and could not move.

Raising my head
to a straw held in front of me
was a challenge.

Maybe I was weighted down
from the blankets.

I was not in pain.

Then I was in pain.

From the simple movement
of scratching
an itch on my nose.

The Mastectomy I Always Wanted

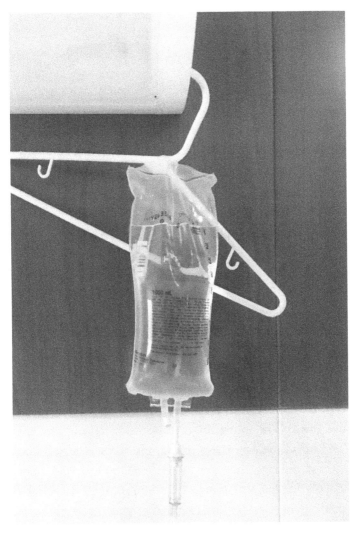

Nothing Is Ever As It Seems . . . or Perfect

Leg Squeezers

I was afraid to move. I lay still like a corpse, with my body surrounded by pillows keeping me motionless. As my consciousness grew, I became aware of two inflatable tubes around my legs from the knees down. No one told me what they were for, and I wondered if I accidentally had surgery on my calves instead. My mind was not working.

The tubes would slowly inflate and squeeze my calves and feet, growing tighter and tighter. I became tortured by another body part that was not my chest. Ten seconds felt like ten minutes. Finally, when I could not bear the pressure for another moment, the air would release in a heavy sigh, and tension disappeared.

For a moment, there was peace. I would think it was over and relax.

Yet the pressure would start up again, startling me. Every round reminded me of a seemingly endless cycle of discomfort. If I managed to sleep, the repetition woke me up. If I was awake, the infuriating pressure clouded my thoughts. The nurse told me these tubes were there to avoid blood clots in my legs from lack of movement, but I wasn't convinced. I was more annoyed by the pressure on my calves than the incisions on my chest. My mind became obsessed with the cycle of madness they created. Watching reality shows on a propped-up laptop was the only distraction that worked. I usually found reality shows a waste of time. However, these were extreme times. In these painful hours, I wanted to watch someone else's wild experiences rather than live my own.

Moving My Arms

I struggled to feed myself. Raising a spoon was a challenge, even though my arms were fine. There were no surgical incisions there. I did not realize how connected chest muscles are to arm movements. I asked a nurse to delicately position the Styrofoam cup of water with a straw right in front of me on the table that extended across the bed frame. My husband had to scratch the itch on my nose for me. I laid back cautiously as if I was paralyzed and frozen.

I requested my husband shove a bunch of pillows around my body like a horseshoe-shaped halo. This created a personal cocoon. I felt safe when I stayed still.

The pain was relentless. Oxycodone did not seem to be working for me. Fundamentally, I did not want to rely on painkillers for fear of addiction, but I needed help. Perhaps I subconsciously desired to feel the pain, but I couldn't articulate why. I wondered if this was the same pain my mom had felt years earlier. Memories of her treatments and surgeries haunted me.

Eventually, I fell asleep thanks to a prescribed combination of Oxycodone and Valium. But when I woke up, I was extremely groggy and confused. My resistance to the repetitive squeezing of my legs grew exponentially. The only way to stop the cycle was to get up and out of bed. My goal was freedom—and that became a powerful motivator.

The Jagged Road to Freedom

After my first night in the hospital, my challenges grew.

Small movements created agonizing pain. I asked my husband to move the water cup close to the edge of the table so I could sip from the straw and stay still. Minor adjustments to my position in bed became a team sport. I needed him to modify the pillows around me with gentle precision. The only way to sit up was with the support of the bed frame, and I preferred someone else to push the buttons on the remote. Lying flat on my back was not an option. The weight of gravity made my upper body ache with pain that felt like a heavy slab of iron burning into my chest.

The nurse encouraged me to try to get out of bed to go to the bathroom. This simple act terrified me. I sat on the edge of the bed with my legs dangling and paused with deep breaths as if I was giving birth. Then, as I leaned into a courageous effort to stand up, I screamed in agony. A sharp, acute pain ripped through my body underneath where my left breast used to be. The nurse froze, and I looked down at my body to see if an invisible knife was cutting me open.

Another nurse arrived, and together they gently peeled back gauze to examine the source as I held my breath. Confused looks washed over their faces. They could not see any tears, redness, or loose objects that could have caused so much visible pain. I walked to the bathroom with an entourage of support and struggled to sit on the toilet. By the time I awkwardly shuffled to bed, I had collapsed in tears. I closed my eyes and imagined being a torture victim. I would have coughed up any secrets for a moment of relief.

Increased pain medicine did not work. The doctor and nurses were confused and unable to provide a clear explanation. The location of the jagged pain was not where any surgical incision occurred. A kind nurse tried alternating warm and cool patches on the spot. The doctor tried to gently massage the area. Nothing worked.

My pain became a mystery.

Typically, a mastectomy patient is discharged after one night. However, the doctor would not release me until they could get the pain under control. I welcomed the extra night in the hospital with mixed emotions. The only path forward given to me was to bear through the pain or wait. I wanted freedom, but I could not comprehend leaving the hospital in my current state.

A Delicate Balance

My body was out of whack. Drain tubes snaked out from under my bandages and captured bloody fluid that built up in my body. I cautiously made minor body movements and tentatively shuffled the ten-step walk to the bathroom. I regressed into a toddler, with an audience cheering on my first few steps and asking if I pooped in the toilet.

I dreaded going to the bathroom. The Oxycodone that was supposed to stop the acute and throbbing pain also hindered my regular bowel movements. In addition to pain management, I needed a first bowel movement to be discharged. Shit needed to happen—literally.

The doctor prescribed a laxative to move along the internal plumbing of my digestive system and free me from possible pain in other parts of my body. I wanted fewer pills and more movement. The irony frustrated me. My body was a delicate balance of pain and progress.

Getting Kicked While I Was Down

Even after my first successful bowel movement, my bathroom activities were closely monitored. The nurses recorded and celebrated every pee and poop. I was less interested in these bathroom habits until I wiped blood from between my legs. Panic shot through my veins, and I freaked out as I stared at the mess and tried to process it. I wondered if blood leaked from my breasts to my bladder. Once the panic subsided, it dawned on me. I burst into tears. My biological clock and hormones didn't care that I had undergone major surgery. I had gotten my period.

Sitting on the toilet, a deep sense of loneliness swept over me. My breasts had already caused me so much pain, and now my uterus was making things worse. I felt like I was being attacked just for being a woman. With a heavy heart, I pressed the call button in the bathroom and spoke to the nurse, my voice choking up with emotion.

She arrived a few minutes later with a tampon and watched. Privacy was gone. I unsuccessfully tried an awkward ballet squat to reach down without bending over. My hands fumbled, and I choked on the rawness of my vulnerability. She offered to help, and I silently nodded. The nurse snapped on surgical gloves, and I spread my legs like a wishbone as she inserted a new tampon.

I ruminated over the irony. I was beginning my menstrual cycle while simultaneously losing my breasts. Life went on. My uterus did not notice what was happening with the rest of my body. I marveled at the masterpiece of the female body and cringed at the despair of the situation. Cramps and extreme humility were added to the list of uncomfortable symptoms.

Getting a tampon in was only half the battle. I realized that what goes in must come out. So every couple of hours, I stood naked in the bathroom while a nurse firmly, yet gently, pulled a tampon out and inserted a new one. Then the drainage bulbs of fluid snaking out from under my bandages were emptied. I felt like blood was oozing out of my body uncontrollably, and I worried about what would come next.

I created a pity party for myself. My body kicked me while I was down, and I wondered if this was payback for some past mistakes. I prayed for relief.

A Visitor

My daughter, Amelia, wanted to visit me. We all agreed that my son, Duncan, was too young to come. He was only five years old. He wouldn't have understood why I couldn't hug or let him crawl into bed with me. While I missed him, the agony of holding back from him seemed too much.

Amelia, on the other hand, was eight years old. The last time we were both in a hospital was when she was born. I wondered about her reaction to such a sterile and unfamiliar experience. My mama bear instinct wanted to shield her from seeing me so helpless, but I knew she would figure it out. She was smart. I intended to appear strong, loving, and unashamed of my body. I didn't want to scare her. Despite the struggles, I wanted her to know that I was still her mom.

Amelia walked into the hospital room with trepidation. She stood next to the bed and asked about the shows on my laptop, the buttons on the bed remote, and the saltine wrappers on the table. She just wanted to be with me.

Food became an easy conversation topic. I was finally hungry, so I let her choose from the cafeteria menu and order whatever sounded good. Cheeseburger, broccoli, rice, applesauce, and a milkshake. When the food was delivered, I gingerly moved to the recliner chair, and we set up a picnic.

My hair was matted and messy after several days without

a shower. Amelia offered to braid my hair to look better. I knew a simple braid wouldn't fix the greasy strands, but I let her try. She wanted to help. I understood the need to do something. I recalled being in the hospital with my mom, too. Mothers and daughters have a special bond.

When I had to go to the bathroom, Amelia went with me. We were inseparable. We sat together, with her on the hospital toilet and me on the portable potty set up so I wouldn't have to squat down. Amelia's legs dangled off the side of the toilet, and we talked. To an outsider, it may have looked strange. But for me, it was perfect. She was my daughter, and we were soul sisters.

The Mastectomy I Always Wanted

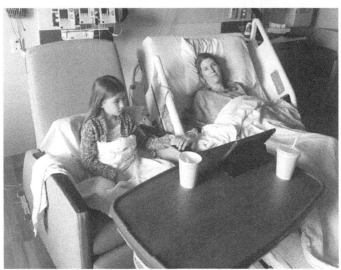

No Rules

The irony of the mastectomy was not lost on me. I was living in my mother's shadow, and the memories of her journey haunted me.

Despite the life-altering grief and sadness from my mom's disease, the good memories remained. When my mom was in the hospital for treatment or complications, I chose to stay overnight with her in the twin bed so I could be close to her and be a resource for any middle-of-the-night issues. During the day, we sorted through old photographs and became good friends with her roommate. When a young MRI technician picked her up in a wheelchair for a routine scan, I encouraged him to pop a wheelie. We often broke the rules.

Now it was my turn.

Until then, my most extensive journey was a short shuffle from my hospital bed to see open windows at the end of the hall. It was all I could muster, and I loved standing before a beautiful gas fireplace along the way. The fire crackled erratically, reminding me that chaos could be calming. I reflected on the experience and what I was learning.

Then it dawned on me. When my mom was in the hospital, we used the opportunity to test our limits together. I wanted to use this experience to honor her and heal myself.

"Let's go break some rules," I told my husband. He didn't

blink at the opportunity to do something different than walk up and down the hallway.

"I want to go further," I said. "On wheels."

Ian got a wheelchair and tucked in blankets from the neck down to protect me from the constant chill. I needed padding to guard me against jostling my body. I didn't want to cause any harm, but I craved a new perspective.

The woman at the nurse's station looked at us with curiosity before returning to her computer screen. "Be safe," she said with a sly smile.

Freedom.

Up until now, the world shrank to the size of my circumstances. This was the first time I had thought about life bigger than these hallways or my hospital room. I was prepared to expand my perspective.

Ian wheeled me around the empty halls, and we searched for rules to break. A hospital can be lonely and quiet after hours. All the hustle and bustle of loved ones, doctors, nurses, and support staff died down as they went home at the end of the day.

We approached the front sliding doors—and saw our mission.

We could see a sunset sky and a world outside the glass walls offering freedom, fresh air, and a large rushing fountain, all waiting to be witnessed at 7:57 p.m. The doors would be locked in three minutes.

The pulse of rule-breaking rose within me. It was time to be free.

Ian pushed me out of the first set of sliding doors, and the exterior ones magically opened. The posted sign warned us about being locked out, which heightened my excitement. I remembered my favorite Virginia Woolf quote from *A Room of One's Own*: "I thought how unpleasant it is to be locked out; and I thought how it is worse, perhaps, to be locked in."

And we left.

Fresh air and freedom touched my soul. Balmy air moisturized my dry skin and welled in my eyes. The last remains of pink fought to stay lit in the late spring sky, dancing with the possibility of the end of a long winter. I could feel the upcoming softness in temperatures and basked in the knowledge that a season of warmth was coming.

Ian pushed me around and around in the wheelchair as we circled the fountain in silence. The simplicity of being in motion, the anticipation in the air, and the breaking of minor rules brought me joy. My healing had begun.

We agreed it was time to return inside when the sun finally disappeared. The darkness let us know it was time to move on. Ian pushed the call button to speak to security. The faceless voice on the other end scolded us for staying out too late. Finally, after a long pause, we heard a shuffling of paper, and the doors slid open. I smiled at Ian.

I delighted in being locked out—because I saw the value of not being locked in. This was the beginning of my freedom. I realized cancer doesn't follow the rules, and neither do I. Cancer creates a level of forgiveness that allows doors to magically open if you wait long enough.

Emerging from the Cocoon

In the middle of the night, a nurse startled me out of my sleep as she flicked on the lights and ripped away my perfectly placed pillows. I screamed in surprise at the sudden and sharp actions, and my husband jumped awake off the pull-out couch in confusion. She was hurrying to take my temperature and blood pressure, which felt like a false alarm for any real urgency. As much as I felt safe being so close to nurses and doctors, the constant sleep interruptions frustrated me. Between the lack of control and the taste of fresh air from the outdoor adventure earlier, I decided it was time to go home.

The cocoon of my life had shrunk into a small hospital room. While I felt unprepared to face the real world, it was time for courage. After that restless night, I agreed to be discharged and prepared to re-enter the world, forever changed. I could not imagine how I would rejoin society and my old life with such an altered state of mind and body, but it was time to find out.

As I prepared for discharge, the nurses gave me detailed instructions on managing the drainage tubes and handed me a strange zip-up vest with front pockets to hold the maroon-filled drainage bulbs. This was supposed to be my new bra for a while. I tried to appear normal, wearing clothes with zippers in the front to conceal my condition. But the truth was, I felt disheveled, weak, and vulnerable. All I longed for was a warm shower and a peaceful night's sleep.

It was now time to heal. I could not see a path forward, so I started with baby steps. The first hurdle was getting into the car with as little movement as possible. The seat belt terrorized me; I didn't want to clip in, let alone have it across my chest. My friend sent me a seat belt cushion with a breast cancer ribbon embroidered on the front. I never believed the money spent on pink ribbon merchandise made a difference, but now was not the time for a boycott.

My joints remained stiff from inactivity. I still felt like a knife was stabbing me under my left breast area. Drainage tubes were tucked under my shirt. But the idea of going home brought resilience. I placed the soft cushion in front of me and gently pushed the seat belt an inch away from my chest for the ten-minute drive home. I closed my eyes in relief at crossing the finish line. Little did I know, the journey was only beginning.

SEVEN

BEGIN AGAIN: TEENAGER 2.0

If you ever get a second chance for something, you've got to go all the way.

— Lance Armstrong

Daily Struggles

The first week at home was a blur of sleep and struggle. My bed did not have the technology to rise and lower with the push of a button. I looked at my old clothes with longing and wonder. My cell phone was full of texts and voicemails. The pain was still acute. And yet the most challenging part was accepting the help I desperately needed.

A loving neighbor mowed my lawn and folded all my laundry. Presents and cards filled my entryway. Friends offered to bring over dinner.

I vacillated between facing reality and pretending to be okay. One morning, Duncan—my beautiful, vibrant, loving son—raced toward me in the kitchen, his face full of excitement and joy. However, I could not even hold a half-gallon of milk due to the pain in my chest muscles from being cut and sewn back together. In addition, the drainage tubes snaked out of my sides, delicately sewn in place. As much as I despised these drains, I did not want them accidentally ripped out of my body. My self-protection mode switched on quickly. As much as I loved Duncan, I inadvertently screamed for him to stay away, holding my hands out to halt him. He stopped in his tracks and crumbled into tears. I cursed myself and apologized profusely, but he did not understand. The delicate balance between protecting my body and protecting his heart broke me.

I craved sleep, but lying flat on my back felt excruciating. I never realized how much chest muscle it took to get in and out of bed—a simple activity I'd taken for granted. To accomplish this now, I required a unique triangle-shaped pillow to elevate my upper body, plus another person pushing on my back to help me sit up. The sheer effort required for such a mundane task became a daunting burden. Desperate to avoid the struggle, I resorted to sleeping in a leather recliner that held me in a comfortable horizontal position. Eventually, I pleaded to move the recliner into our bedroom to avoid dozing off in the living room. This old leather chair became my favorite place in the house—a haven of solace and relief from the constant burden of daily life.

Showering was another temptation out of my grasp. Over the last few days, I found sticky spots in strange places on my body, which I assumed were where heart rate sensors or other surgical monitoring devices were taped to me. My body smelled of peroxide and rubbing alcohol. The grease in my hair started to itch. My surgeon only allowed me to wipe my body with a wet washcloth.

I clung to any moments of happiness that came my way.

Even though I didn't want presents, well-meaning friends sent gifts in the mail or dropped them on our doorstep. My house quickly became cluttered and overwhelming. However, a group of thoughtful friends came up with a unique idea to send me a picture instead. I was deeply touched that they had taken the time to coordinate such a heartfelt and personal gift. It was a reminder that they were thinking of me. This simple gesture became the most cherished gift of all.

Moving Along

If you saw me from afar, you would never suspect I had undergone a mastectomy so recently. I was a mastectomy spy in disguise. With some baggy tops, I looked normal. I avoided clothes where I needed to raise my arms or pull over my head. Before surgery, my husband purchased at least ten cheap tops that opened in the front or pulled up from my waist. As a result, my wardrobe became limited, but at least I was out of my pajamas.

After the first week, I finally got clearance from my doctor to shower. He gave me safety instructions and encouraged me to gently move my upper body using the relief of steam and warm water. I couldn't wait to shower and remove the hospital aura that haunted me. But a tiny terror held me back. As I stood naked and waited for the water to heat up, I was not convinced I was ready. I wondered if the pelting of water would hurt. I worried about the drain tubes hanging delicately by cheap lanyard string around my neck like a heavy necklace. But I stepped in and turned my back to the showerhead, only letting the warmth fall slowly over my shoulders onto my chest. That was enough to comfort me and wash away some anxiety. I conquered my first milestone alone.

However, the shower also had a downside. It made me

look better, but the reality was that I was far from fine. Sadly, people seemed to forget my struggle quickly. I knew this was not intentional, but I felt lonely and invisible. I wished I could easily forget, but it wasn't always that simple.

My husband and kids asked if I wanted to go to a lake property for a long weekend. Going to this cabin meant lots of neighbors, food, and wine. While this was usually a great place to relax and forget the daily grind, I would have to leave the comforts of home behind. My children would expect me to play in the sand along the lakeshore and run into the water. With a buzz of parenting, people, and activities, I knew my recovery would be easily overlooked.

As I wrestled with the dilemma of leaving the safety of my home, a sudden realization hit me like a bolt of lightning—the leather recliner was easily disassembled. I remembered how we had purchased the chair from an online neighborhood listing and unhooked the latches in the back to fit it into our small SUV.

When my husband entered the bedroom to check on me as I packed, I tentatively proposed bringing the recliner to the cabin. To my great relief, he readily agreed. The simple act of taking this old leather chair with us became a beacon of hope, providing me the promise of a small but meaningful piece of home away from home. With this token of support, I reluctantly agreed to go.

The car trunk was packed like a jigsaw puzzle, but my husband made it work. As a family unit, we all made compromises. Kids were squished in the backseat, and I gingerly sat in the front with my seatbelt pillow. I found a way to be both a healer for myself and a mom who could still travel.

Normalcy

At the cabin, I felt the pain of normalcy slip through my fingers. I wanted the old me back sooner than my body and mind allowed. Being on the boat for a ride across the lake was deeply challenging. I smiled with clenched teeth and faked it the whole time. Every jostling from the waves brought an extra reminder of the surgery and the drain tubes. It became exhausting to keep pretending. Although I tried to rest, the kids rightfully wanted me near them. I kept pushing through to blend in and appear happy. Despite being around so many people, my loneliness grew and overtook me. When I snuck away to be alone, the relief came from rest and letting go of expectations to return to my old self so quickly.

The Mastectomy I Always Wanted

The Longest Yard

I fought a daily mental battle against the drain tubes, recognizing they were there for a good reason but struggling against extreme discomfort. I felt like an invasive species of snakes had invaded my body and burrowed deep. The blood and fluid from the surgery needed to drain from my body, and this was the only way out. I needed to protect these tubes like delicate butterflies, but I also wanted to rip them out. They were a necessary evil.

Every four hours, I needed another person to change the dressing, empty the bulbs that collected blood and fluid, and measure the contents. I reminded myself that the foreign objects inside and outside of me were supposed to help, not harm. The changes in my body were under close surveillance, unfamiliar and messy. It reminded me of the first few days after childbirth when my body was utterly out of whack while managing a new life. Each day was a struggle to maintain sanity.

I counted the days until my scheduled removal of the drain tubes as if it was the end of my prison sentence. While at the cabin and fighting to keep sanity, the surgeon's office called unexpectedly. The scheduling assistant asked to postpone my appointment to remove my drainage tubes until next week to accommodate the long Memorial Day holiday weekend. The idea of waiting five more days seemed like five more years. This meant extending my mental survival timeline. I wasn't sure I could make it another hour with these awful snakes coming out of my body. I broke into tears.

A phrase in football called "the longest yard" is when a team faces unsurmountable odds to get to the goal line. They fight hard to move the ball forward an inch in the face of inexperience, self-doubt, and unexpected attacks.

This was my longest yard. I could see the finish line, but the goalposts kept moving farther away.

The drain tubes were my delicate demons. This tension wore on me in ways I could not explain to myself or others. I inched forward despite the setback and turned inward to find resilience from a deep reserve. I felt like my mental game had just gone into overtime, so I brought reinforcements. The underdog in me would not back down. I listened to empowering music to strengthen my soul. I let powerful lyrics sink into my bones and fuel me. I put up walls to defend myself and protect my thoughts. The raw parts of me were exposed, so I avoided being seen. During these last five days, I could not look down at what was happening with my chest.

Erica Neubert Campbell

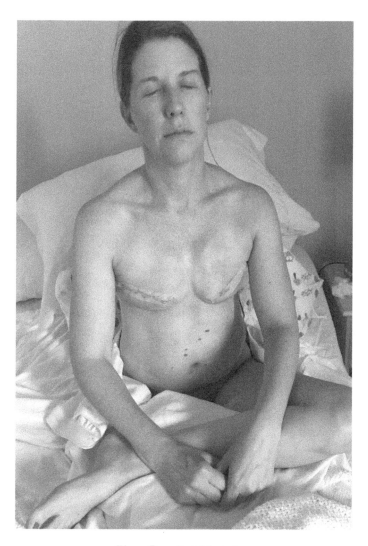

Eleven Days Post-Mastectomy

Seismic Relief

After over two weeks of insane amounts of resilience and grit, the time came to have the drain tubes removed. The nurse clipped a few external stitches under my armpit and told me to breathe deeply. Then, she tugged gently but forcefully on the lines as if pulling the escape cord on a parachute. When I saw the length of the tubes previously inside me, I was disgusted. They were longer and thicker than I expected. I had defeated a beast without knowing the size of the monster. A wave of seismic relief washed over me as I left the treatment room.

This feeling of freedom flooded my veins and fueled a bit of pride. Although pain remained, the extreme discomfort was gone. I recognized that this freedom would bring new possibilities and new challenges. I was like a boxer who had won the first match. I took a few hard punches, yet I returned to the ring. The world was shifting. My yoga teacher was right. The real work was beginning. Without the drain tubes, I also lost the ability to complain about them. I was being gently nudged back into real life, and this realization became a mind game.

Normalcy is a choice. Later that day, I decided to return as a soccer mom to my son. My husband brought a lawn chair to the game, and I needed help sitting down. I was

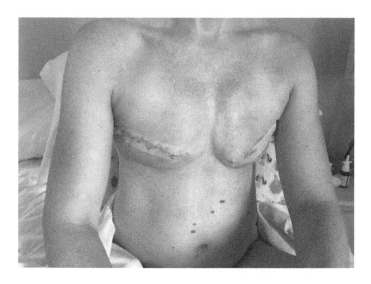

literally on the sidelines. I hid my pain, made small talk with other parents, and lightly hugged my son. The world buzzed around me, and I began to re-enter my life.

The Mastectomy I Always Wanted

Fourteen Days Post-Mastectomy

Everyday Badass

An acquaintance at work brought me a gift based on the story of my post-mastectomy power statement. Because she knew I could not remember what I had said about myself, she gave me this bracelet to remember. I was a badass every day. This feeling became my personal mantra. I had said it unconsciously, and now I could bring it into my daily awareness. From that point forward, I wore the bracelet every day. The gratitude for small acts of kindness overwhelmed me.

Undercover Frankenstein

After a few weeks, my doctor began discussing the start of saline injections. The speed of this transition surprised me. I still had a Frankenstein-looking chest. Although monsters never scared me, the idea of moving forward frightened me. More needles were ahead.

During the mastectomy surgery, my natural breasts were replaced with "expanders," which were described to me as two deflated balloons under my skin. I started flat and empty. These expanders intended to slowly stretch my chest muscles and skin to build a pocket for permanent breast implants to be swapped out later. The plan was to inject a saline solution in small increments over several appointments and slowly fill the balloons to make new breasts. At the start of each fill session, a nurse held a magnet to my skin to find the correct injection site and marked the spot. With metal in my body, I felt like a defeated superhero returning from war with battle scars and artificial limbs. I was being rebuilt with spare parts. At times, I fought against the feeling that I was creating something unnatural, but the visible growth gave me the grit to keep going.

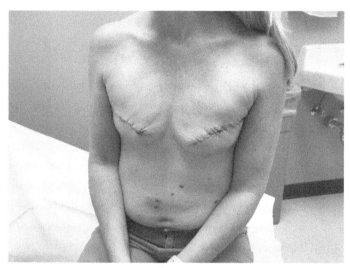
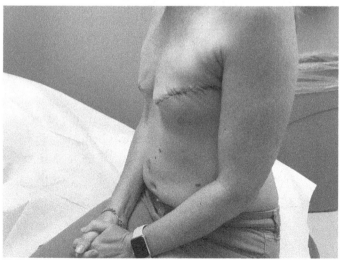

Twenty Days Post-Mastectomy

Gratitude

Continuous forward progress is contagious. Every baby step led to more confidence for the next one. I became grateful for the little moments I might have missed. Cuddling became possible again. In my bed, I slept with a complicated routine of pillows. With my kids, I used their love and stuffed animals to comfort me.

A Trust Hangover

As time moved away from acute fears and limits, a roller coaster of emotions flooded in. I wanted to know what had happened during the six-hour surgery. My last memory before the anesthesia was lying on a table in a large white room with at least a dozen nurses and attendants staring at me.

I made up stories in my head about that time. I contemplated the human needs of each doctor or nurse. Over the six hours, at least one person's mind would have wandered. Maybe one of the nurses was having a bad day. Had they been talking about the latest Netflix movies while I'd been lying there, breasts wide open and unaware? Did I bleed uncontrollably and stain the floor? Was the knife sharp enough? Did someone get hungry and step away to shove a granola bar into their mouth? Did my doctor make jokes with the nursing team? Were they playing music? And if so, was it heavy metal or Taylor Swift? Did they take a selfie with my limp, heavy body?

I believed in the integrity of the doctors, nurses, and care team. And yet I struggled with the stories in my head. The level of trust I needed exceeded my original limits. As a woman who likes to control, I struggled with the knowledge that during those six hours, I had no conscious awareness of how my body was handled. At a weekly appointment,

I awkwardly asked my doctor about the actual process of cutting skin and what veins were cut. While he answered my clinical questions, he gently encouraged me to let it go. The answers to these questions wouldn't give me control. His compassion made me feel safe, yet these questions lingered in my brain. It was like a trust hangover that took weeks to recover.

I also questioned my decisions about the next step. My current pain was directly related to my choice to insert implants under my chest muscle. I started to like being slightly flat-chested. I looked thinner from the immediate loss of a few pounds of flesh. With this new lightness, I wondered if I'd made the wrong decision to pursue implants and reconstruction. What I saw in the mirror started to look good enough. The subsequent surgery to replace the expanders with permanent implants loomed large.

I knew breast reconstruction was the right path, but I grew weary of the uncertainty and doubt. I thought the initial surgery meant the end of the decisions, but I was wrong. More choices loomed. Now I faced the size and shape of my new fake breasts, the type of implant, and the volume of saline. Whenever I questioned the next step or the pace of my progress, my doctor asked me to trust him. And I did.

Four Weeks Post-Mastectomy

The Wisdom That Comes with Age

I decided to reframe the experience as the chance to be a teenager again. However, this time I would get to pick the size and shape of my growing breasts and watch it all happen on fast-forward. The doctor allowed me to choose how much saline he injected into the expanders based on my desired growth progress and pain tolerance. At each injection, the fluid grew inside the balloon under my chest and stretched my skin with a dull ache, like getting your braces tightened at the orthodontist.

Despite the discomfort, at least I had control. This time, I got to look at myself in the mirror with pride and compassion rather than embarrassment. Whenever I felt self-conscious, I reminded myself that the awkwardness would pass. The opportunity to approach the changes in my body with power was affirming. I examined my breasts in the mirror with wonder and curiosity.

There is wisdom that comes with age. I experienced a difference inside and out. I was regrowing my body and becoming at peace with the changes.

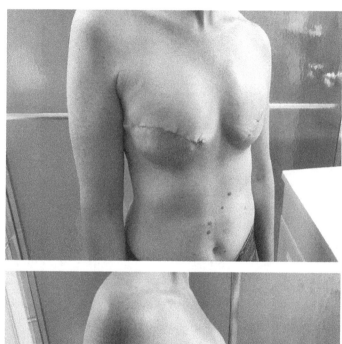
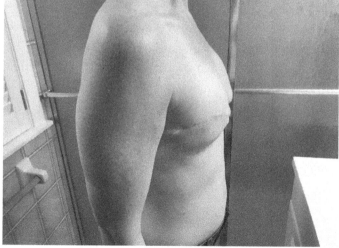

Five Weeks Post-Mastectomy

HEALERS

I leaned into sunsets and time. Both healed. I was still flat-chested but stronger and back on the boat.

Getting into nature helped tremendously. Sunsets reminded me of the beauty in endings. Water reminded me that life can be both choppy and calm in the same season. Summer felt warm on my chest.

When my mom died, several people told me that time would heal my wounds. I desperately hated that phrase. At the time, it felt like a backhand comment to my pain. Now here I was having to admit that time healed. Wisdom and joy were blending into feelings of hope.

Six Weeks Post-Mastectomy

Becoming CEO

Life went on. The regular cadence of bills to pay, kid activities, and appointments carried on. A few weeks after my breast surgery, I had my annual visit to the dermatologist. I found myself sitting on the exam table with my legs dangling and feeling a bit tired of doctor appointments. The primary reason for the visit was a routine check of the moles on my skin. But naturally, I showed her my breast scars. She observed them carefully and confirmed what my plastic surgeon told me: my new breasts would be beautiful.

I struggled to believe her. My chest looked like Frankenstein on a bad day, sewn together with big, ugly stitches. She complimented the work and assured me my scars would heal. My dermatologist had the conviction and faith I lacked. I couldn't see what she saw, but I trusted her experience. A seed of hope was planted.

However, I was taken off guard a few days later when she called me with unfortunate news. She sighed as she told me my test results discovered a cancerous mole on my stomach. All I heard was the "cancer" word. The administrative staff quickly scheduled another surgery to remove early-stage skin cancer.

Immediately, the thought of more body parts being removed sent me into deep despair. I wondered if doctors were slowly going to cut away all of me—or if cancer would kill me one way or another. When I returned to the dermatologist, I was so overwhelmed that I could barely speak before I sobbed into my hands.

After I calmed down and wiped the messy tears from my face, she encouraged me to look at this situation differently. Her perspective was that I was proactive with regular screening and early detection. She reminded me that both my cancers were caught early. I avoided massive cancer scares before they developed. She believed I was ahead of the game. I liked that story better and did my best to stay positive. The mole was removed with deep cuts, and I left with stitches and bandages.

A week later, I faced yet another surprise. My plastic surgeon was deeply upset when he noticed the bandage on my stomach at my check-up appointment. He worried that this mole removal procedure on my abdomen could have caused an infection. This was not on my laundry list of worries. He explained the big problems women faced from complications after surgery. It had never crossed my mind to worry about infection. I left his office debating the balance between known and unknown risks.

While this surgery was a physical experience, it was equally a mental game of mind over matter. I realized how much I chose to create my reality. I accepted the risk of surgery—with and without knowing the dangers. I trusted myself and my decisions. I achieved each milestone with resilience and determination. I was becoming the chief executive officer of my health.

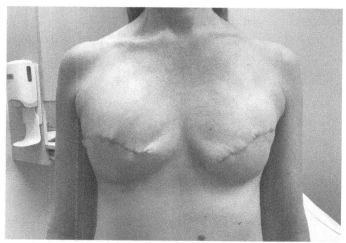

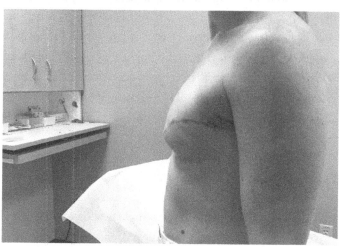

The Mastectomy I Always Wanted

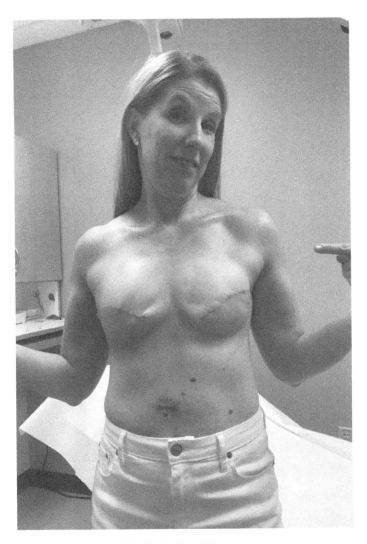

Eight Weeks Post-Mastectomy

Growth

My breasts grew bigger every two weeks, and the healing accelerated. At my next saline injection appointment, the nurse told me to rub lotions vigorously into the scars. She reached over and demonstrated the intensity. This was not her first rodeo. The amount of pressure felt unnatural, but I knew she was an experienced professional. I vowed to stretch my own limiting beliefs about what I could handle.

My breasts were lumpy, and every nurse assured me I was on the right path. They told me how good my breasts would look when this was over. I sincerely wanted to believe them. The scars looked like ripped-up windshield wipers, but my chest started to take shape. Finally, my eyes were beginning to see what they were seeing.

The Mastectomy I Always Wanted

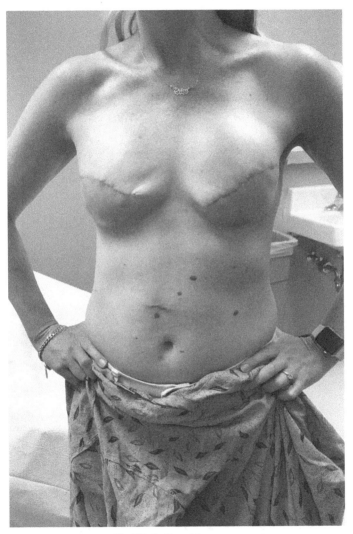

Ten Weeks Post-Mastectomy

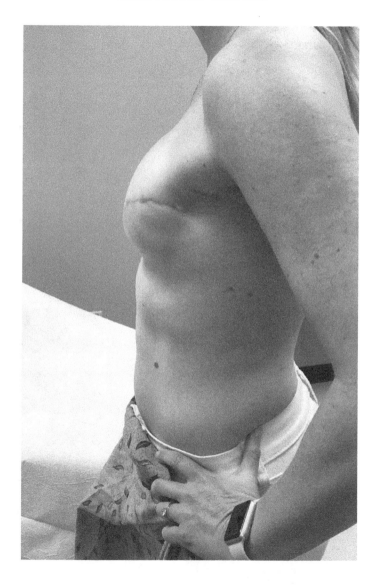

The Goal

At each appointment, I was allowed to decide how much saline to be injected into the breast expanders. I was back in the driver's seat of my journey. I got to choose the speed of growth based on my tolerance level and desire for progress.

At the start of this phase, Ian and I set a clear goal with my doctor. We wanted to finish the injections before our trip to Indonesia for a wedding in a few months. The idea of traveling halfway around the world only three months after the most extensive surgery of my life seemed absurd. I did not think I would be well enough to travel. My husband asked questions about timing, the volume of saline, and the risks involved. I asked questions about traveling so far from home, wearing a backpack, and getting through airport security with metal implanted under my skin.

I waded through the doubts and insecurities but stuck to the vision. I wanted to be that person who showed up in the face of fear. Although the pace felt faster than my comfort level, I knew change was coming.

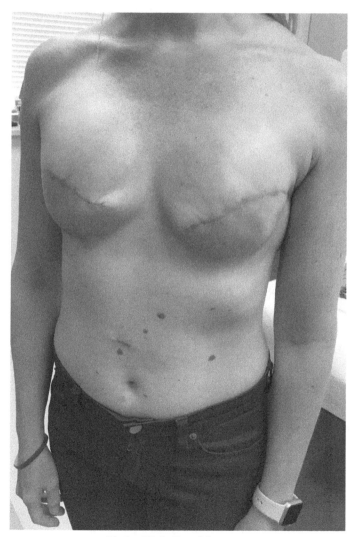

Twelve Weeks Post-Mastectomy

The Mastectomy I Always Wanted

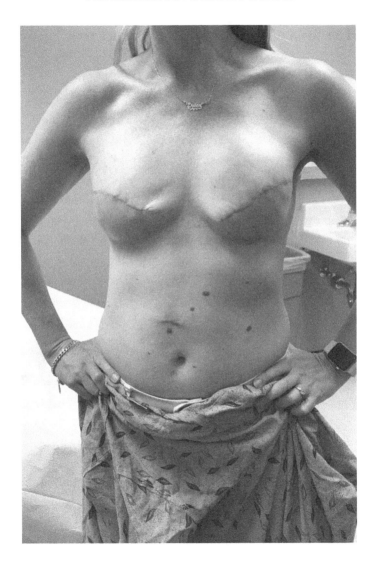

Halfway Around the World

After massive trepidation, minimalist packing, and a healthy dose of courage, we made it to Indonesia for the wedding!

I fought back the tears at airport security with every leg of the journey. As I approached each security checkpoint, I scanned the officers to determine who looked the kindest. With a soft voice and humble heart, I explained that metal was in my breasts, so I could not go through the metal detector. When language was a barrier, I pointed at my chest and the sign about implants, which typically meant a heart pacemaker. At one airport, a female officer gave me a full pat down. Another time, a security officer nodded in acceptance after the sensors went off. I slowed down the lines and received curious stares from other passengers.

At the wedding, I wore the same dress I had worn years before the surgery. The only difference was that I didn't need a bra this time. My fake breasts held up on their own. I started to see the silver lining. I no longer needed the profound release of a tight strapless bra at the end of a long night.

I found it ironic that I needed to go halfway around the world to feel in control of my journey. As with everything in life, there was always further to go. I began to relax. We did yoga by the sea. The irony was not lost on me. The scenery and the thrill of travel inspired me. I was doing what most people would consider ridiculous.

On the last day of our trip, my husband convinced me to swim in the ocean despite my fears of the big waves and turbulence. We held on to each other dearly, keeping our heads above water. The saltwater and the strength of our partnership softened my internal and external wounds.

Erica Neubert Campbell

Thirteen Weeks Post-Mastectomy

The Mastectomy I Always Wanted

Rebirth

After the trip, I had to hurry up and wait. My only job was to let my skin settle, stretch, and heal for three months until the next surgery. We celebrated my forty-fifth birthday, met with my doctor, and scheduled the surgery to replace the expanders with long-term implants. Happy rebirth to me and my boobs!

The Mastectomy I Always Wanted

Fifteen Weeks Post-Mastectomy—and My Forty-Fifth Birthday

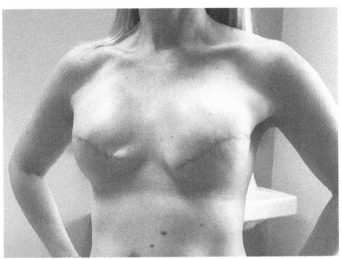

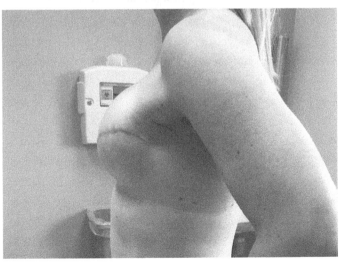

A Silver Lining

The day before the surgery to swap out the expanders with the "permanent" set of breast implants was filled with mixed emotions. I was nervous about another surgery. The first one hadn't been fun. However, my plastic surgeon assured me this second surgery would not be like the first.

This upcoming surgery would be outpatient, meaning I would arrive early in the morning and leave by noon the same day. The quick turnaround seemed impossible. The fears associated with surgery began to rise again. While I knew the next step was necessary, I considered postponing or canceling. The mental game was exhausting.

Over the last few months, I grew comfortable with the status quo. I had accepted these expanders and did not want to change my body again. I moved back into the regular cadence of life as a mom, wife, and leader. I inadvertently forgot about the next surgery without weekly doctor appointments and saline injections.

Denial had become a steady crutch, and the months drifted into comfortable routines. I didn't want to disrupt the rhythms of life I had re-created. The idea of an additional surgery felt like two steps back. But deep down, I understood that change is both essential and inevitable. Despite my hesitation, I agreed to move forward with this replacement surgery. I had to go through the discomfort to get fake boobs forever. I suspected there was a silver lining to be found.

The Replacements

During my pre-surgical consultation, I learned liposuction was part of the standard protocol for expander replacement surgery. The surgeon would insert a catheter below my belly button to transfer fat from my stomach to the gaps around the breast implant. A "fat graft" would make my permanent fake breasts look more natural. I was delighted by the idea of removing belly fat as part of the required process of this surgery. New boobs and a smaller waist at the same time! Jackpot!

Naturally, I made a joke. I begged the doctor to keep the liposuction machine on a bit longer after he removed the necessary fat needed for my breasts. He laughed, even though I'm sure he had heard this request from every woman before me. If I was going to have required liposuction, I wanted it all. Go big or go home, I thought.

THE MASTECTOMY I ALWAYS WANTED

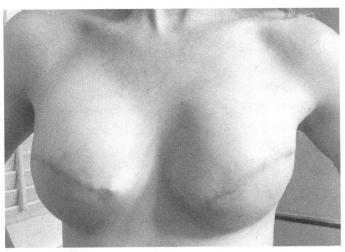

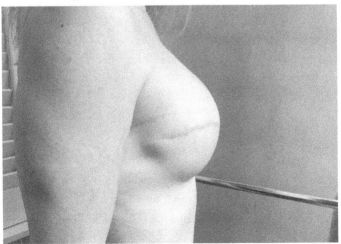

*Six Months Post-Mastectomy
and the Day before the Expander Replacement Surgery*

What Happened to the "Easy" Button?

On the morning of the procedure, I started with a positive mindset. I imagined an easy recovery, an enhanced set of breasts, and a smaller waist. Everything seemed on track for a better life, and I strolled into the surgery center with a nervous swagger.

However, as I stripped down to a paper robe and they inserted the IV into my arm, the positive vibes tumbled away. I began to panic. The feelings and fears from my mastectomy resurfaced and took my breath away. Despite logically knowing these were different surgeries, the similarities in the preparation raised my blood pressure, and I began to shiver. The surgeon and the anesthesiologist came by with calm, reassuring words that I could not hear. Fear took over, and I was whisked away to be put to sleep so they could get to work.

I woke up groggy and nauseous, with bandages across my chest and a girdle fastened around my waist. The only external evidence of liposuction was a small bandage over my belly button, but the internal discomfort made it hard to breathe. I tried to rest and close my eyes, but the nurses insisted I could go home. My abs felt like a shredded tire that ran over nails. I wobbled as I stood up from the wheelchair and lowered myself into our car. As I laid my head back on the neck rest, I wondered what had happened to me.

When I got home, I did not want to look at the results in the mirror. The postsurgical bruises and swelling startled me. My breasts were obscenely swollen and bloated, and my stomach wailed with discomfort. So many people told me this would be an "easy" surgery. Unfortunately, that was not my experience. I looked like I got into a fistfight with a breast criminal. My chest cup size seemed to have doubled in size. The results were almost comical. It hurt to laugh, especially with such sore abdominals.

Yes, I looked like boob ninjas had assaulted me, but I realized the worst was over. I had been broken and bruised before. My resilience muscles flexed again as I hobbled around my house and needed help with basic tasks. I took my advice and rested. Although my body was in pain, my fear was lighter. I found peace in knowing the final surgery was behind me. I no longer wore the backpack of worry.

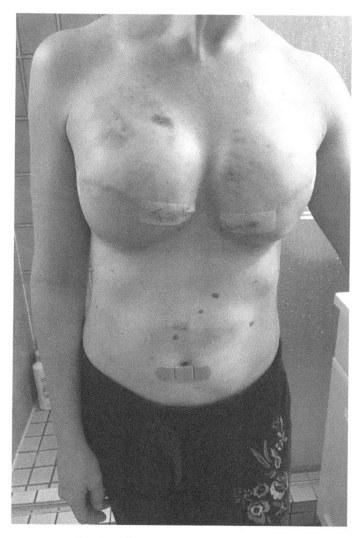

One Day after Expander Replacement Surgery

Pulling My Shit Together

Two weeks after my expander replacement surgery, my recovery accelerated. I booked a trip to visit my best friend, Kate, and her husband, who lived in San Francisco. Kate and I have been friends since college, and I was sure her perspective would be healing. I knew that friendship through highs and lows was the secret sauce of my life. Kate and I were roommates for years, and she was one of the first people I turned to when my mom died. I brought my newborn son to her wedding. Kate had seen my original breasts multiple times through good times and bad. Going back to my roots seemed the best way to move forward.

When I arrived, Kate gave me a T-shirt. She was the master of the perfect gift. The quote on the front was from the icon Elizabeth Taylor. "Pour yourself a drink, put on some lipstick, and pull your shit together." This is precisely what I did.

Over the weekend, we drank wine, ate soul-filling foods, and dove into laughter and memories. I borrowed her leopard print coat and her positive attitude. When I showed Kate my new breasts, she squealed with delight. She saw the beauty in my cancer-free life and the firmness of my perky breasts. We laughed over the age reversal of my "new rack." Her outlook shifted my perspective on the results of this latest surgery. Kate was always known for her sense of fashion and self-compassion.

I arrived in San Francisco feeling ugly and bruised under the surface. But I left feeling fabulous inside and out. Kate was the mirror I needed to see the true joy in my progress.

Two Weeks After My Expander Replacement Surgery

Affirmations

As time passed after my expander replacement implant surgery, my mind cleared. I did not realize how much the weight of expectation had been holding me back. Looking in the rearview mirror, the anticipation of the expander replacement surgery was worse than the actual surgery.

As the end of the calendar year approached, I reflected on the highs and lows. My confidence grew in surviving the worst months of my life. I created new affirmations to focus my mind.

I'm healing.

I'm lighter and stronger.

I'm ready for a new year.

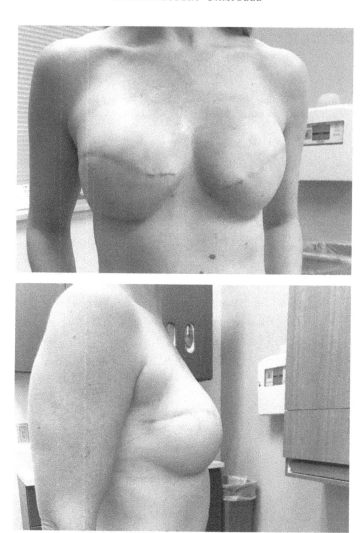

One Month after Expander Replacement Surgery

Ready to Fly

A month after the surgery to replace the expanders, I started weekly physical therapy to work through the new scars and limitations. Because I already worked with this therapist after my first surgery, starting over felt like one step forward and two steps back. Each visit, the physical therapist would push, pull, and massage my breast tissue, armpit, and chest muscles like she was tenderizing a chicken cutlet. She did not hold back. I laid down on a flat table, topless, and she would raise my arm over my head. She approached the process with precision and clinical knowledge. Where I was hesitant, she was confident. I walked out hopeful. The soreness was tangible, but I appreciated the discomfort. It was the pain of slow and steady progress.

Between sessions, my homework was to lather on heavy moisturizer and massage the scars and skin tissue. I followed her instructions like a star student. After three months, I could fully reach my arms toward the sky again. She encouraged me to go back to the gym and try a push-up. The only restrictions were the ones I placed on myself. I didn't believe it was possible, but she kept insisting I try. After a few attempts, I understood she was right.

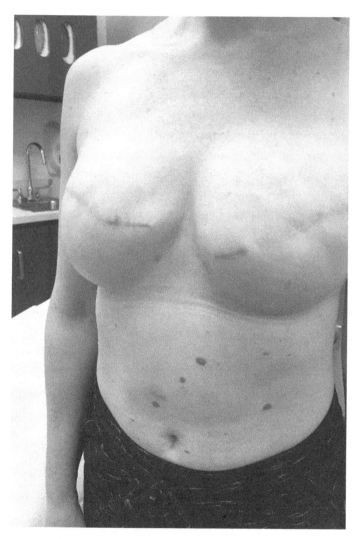

Three Months after the Expander Replacement Surgery

The Mastectomy I Always Wanted

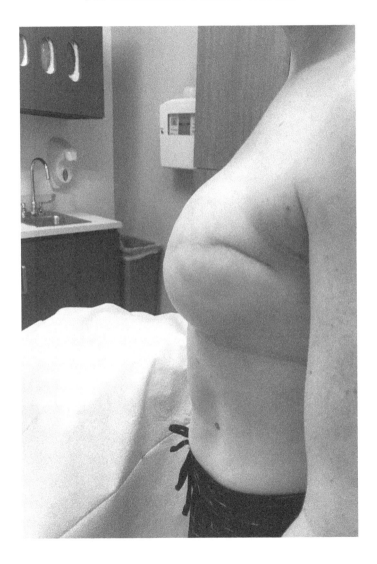

ERICA NEUBERT CAMPBELL

One Year Post-Mastectomy

One Year Later

Exactly one year after my mastectomy, I escaped to an off-site leadership retreat away from family, work, and the daily grind. During the afternoon free time, I deeply reflected on the year. What a wild journey from lying helpless in a hospital gurney to traveling solo with the windows down and belting inspirational songs in my car. The whirlwind of life over the last year flashed before my eyes, and I did not want to let it pass without capturing the lessons. I sat alone in my hotel room and wrote letters to my children for them to read when they are older. I journaled about the highs and lows that marked the last year. Then I ventured into nature to be inspired and grounded.

I originally came out of surgery with my world flipped upside down, leaving me confused and vulnerable. But over the last twelve months, I chose to take control of my life and turn things around. I had been working physically and mentally on my recovery. My goal was to get back to a new normal. I had been practicing and strengthening to do a handstand again. While on a walk, I decided to mark my progress. As I held a perfect yoga handstand, I felt a sense of triumph and pride wash over me.

Looking back, I realized the slow rise of my strength and determination. Though my life had been forever altered, I refused to give up. Instead, I trusted the process and allowed myself to change in unexpected ways.

Even when I felt weak and powerless, I pushed myself to new heights and achieved things I never thought possible, like holding a handstand long enough to snap a photo with a self-timer. Today, I stood tall and proud, a testament to my grit and resilience.

Life is funny that way. Until then, I had discounted the baby steps and micro-progress in the valley of life. As I reflected on the last year, I remembered that I initially could not itch my nose by myself. Today I bore the strength to do a handstand. I persevered even when life was turned upside down. The myriad of decisions and progress flashed like a slideshow in my mind. I underestimated the power of trust, hope, and determination until now.

Lasering

I progressed quickly as I continued my healing process and regular check-ins. My upper body strength returned, and the physical therapy sessions eventually ended. However, despite the improvements, the scars continued to bother me. There was a visible discrepancy between what I saw in the mirror and my desire for normalcy. The lingering scars across my breasts were a constant reminder of the incisions made with sharp knives, and it was hard for me to come to terms with it. My impatience grew, and I wished the scars would disappear.

Based on my doctor's encouragement, I scheduled laser treatments to reduce the appearance of the scars. I had no idea what to expect. During each session, I wore protective goggles while a nurse shot sparks of light onto the scar line. I closed my eyes and pretended I was a droid from a Star Wars movie being soldered together. The nurse practitioner would move from left to right, creating sparks that left tiny burn marks in a dotted pattern across my breast scars. The process took less than five minutes, and I walked out with a line of small red dots that looked like miniature fireworks exploded along the scars. The spots would fade within a week, and the scar would improve. Progress was slow but steady, which became the metaphor for my life.

ERICA NEUBERT CAMPBELL

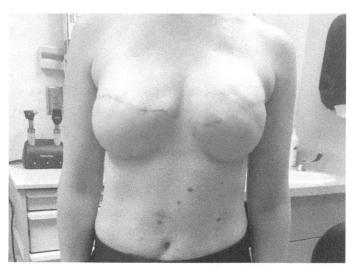

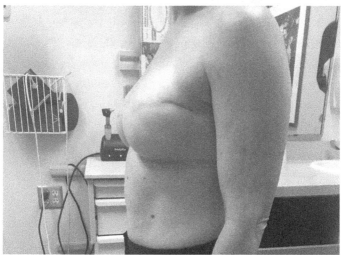

Thirteen Months Post-Mastectomy

Hitting the Pause Button

I kept lasering, massaging, and wishing the scars away. I lathered on shea butter moisturizer during the day and applied scar strips at night. However, an uneasy feeling grew inside me. Despite my attempts to force the healing process, there was a nagging feeling of incompletion.

The next step was to consider a nipple tattoo. I scheduled a consultation with the nurse practitioner at my plastic surgeon's office. We talked about the nipple replacement options and reviewed pictures of her work. At the end of the consultation, I booked an appointment to have the tattoo done at the doctor's office.

But it didn't stick. Instead, a gnawing feeling of incompleteness and avoidance grew.

The day before the procedure, I spontaneously called the office to cancel. After I hung up the phone, I sat in my car and closed my eyes. Relief washed over me, but another emotion followed that left me confused. Something was stopping me.

I wondered if the lingering scars represented something invisible in my heart. This was not about my appearance. I heard a little voice inside me saying I wasn't ready to close the chapter yet. I took several deep breaths and waited.

I could no longer avoid the doubts, fears, and hurts from my prior experiences.

I decided I would not move forward with the final physical step of the journey until I completed the emotional healing. I avoided this road long enough. My next phone call was to a mental health therapist specializing in breast cancer patients. The hardest part was making the call to set the appointment. After that hurdle, the process fell into place.

I met with a counselor every two weeks for the next several months. Her gentle demeanor and welcoming space melted my resistance. Over time, I let go of the stigma around needing support and looked forward to our sessions.

Talking through the deeply held fears was terrifying but ultimately freeing. She gently encouraged me to say everything I thought was too scary to admit. I learned to be comfortable with uncomfortable emotions. While we spoke about my breast cancer and the surgeries, we ventured into topics around my mother's death and the challenges of being a mom. She held up a mirror to my limiting beliefs about my future by asking powerful yet simple questions. I found acceptance, understanding, and a deep release of bottled-up emotions. Underneath my breasts was my heart.

We also discussed my enormous fear of cancer coming back. I knew many people who celebrated the end of their cancer journey only to relapse years later. My mind wandered into the worst-case scenarios when I heard cancer stories. She reminded me that every cancer journey is unique, and cancer is not the end. Whenever I heard about a relapse or a new diagnosis from someone I knew, I repeated a simple mantra: "That's not my story." With this mantra, I could still feel compassion for their diagnosis and remind myself that their cancer would not necessarily be mine. She gave me powerful tools to remember that I am unique and writing my own story.

After we uncovered and released my fears of the past and the future, we discussed a plan to get closure on my journey. I wanted the freedom to be me as I approached the next step. She helped me identify my desire to celebrate and have fun with my tattoos. While I liked the nurse practitioner at my plastic surgeon's office, I wanted more fanfare. Finally, something sparked in my brain, and I started to dream big.

I wrapped up with my therapist with much more clarity, peace, and calmness. She healed in ways no one could see, but I could feel. Visible and invisible scars were finally fading.

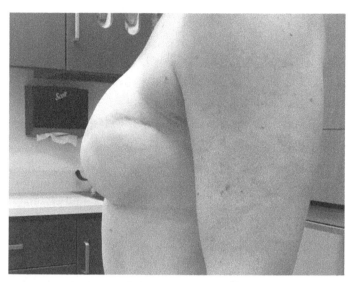
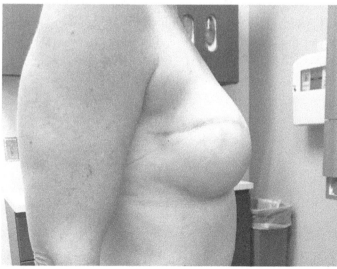

The Mastectomy I Always Wanted

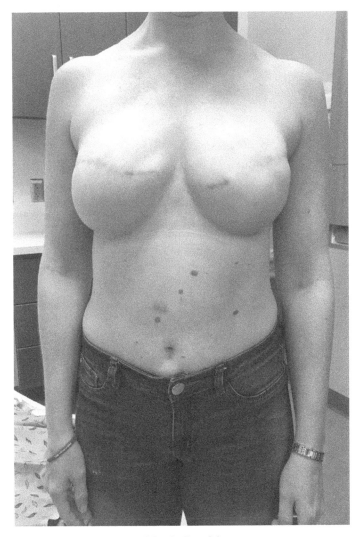

Fourteen Months Post-Mastectomy

EIGHT

INKED

My body is my journal, and my tattoos are my story.

— Johnny Depp

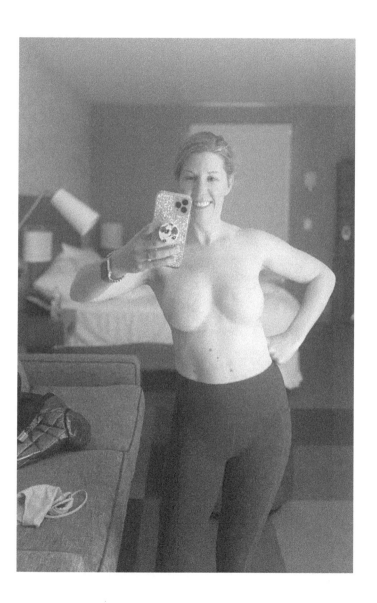

Full Circle

If I was going to get the tattoo, I wanted to do it right. An interesting article in *People Magazine* about a famous breast nipple tattoo artist caught my eye. I wanted to be a celebrity in my own right, so I called and spontaneously booked an appointment. Yes, I trusted *People Magazine* to decide how my breasts would look for the rest of my life.

The closest I ever got to a permanent tattoo was when I spent the summer after college as a camp counselor. I planned to get the female symbol inked in the center of my lower back to represent feminism and strength. But as I walked into the tattoo parlor, I saw the needles, the pain, and the messiness, and I chickened out. I left with my metaphorical tail between my legs. I remained feminist in my heart but not on my lower back. I was afraid of permanence and pain.

Until now. Oh, the irony. Nearly twenty-five years later, I was begging for a tattoo to mark me as feminine again.

The night before my appointment, I spent the evening with my best girlfriends who lived nearby. They treated me like a celebrity. Everyone came out to see my boobs and wish me well. They gave me a meaningful necklace that had a symbol of friendship as well as the pink-rhinestone ribbon of breast cancer. This gift moved me to tears. I sincerely knew this was the right place and the right decision.

Given the COVID-19 pandemic, I stayed in a hotel and got to be by myself to mark this last chapter. On the morning of the appointment, I took pictures of my blank breasts without nipples with a renewed sense of pride and empowerment. This had been such a long time coming. I was finally at the goal line, ready to score a new set of boobs.

I was not going back to an old version of myself. I realized that was impossible. I was creating the new me, and I liked this one better.

The Mastectomy I Always Wanted

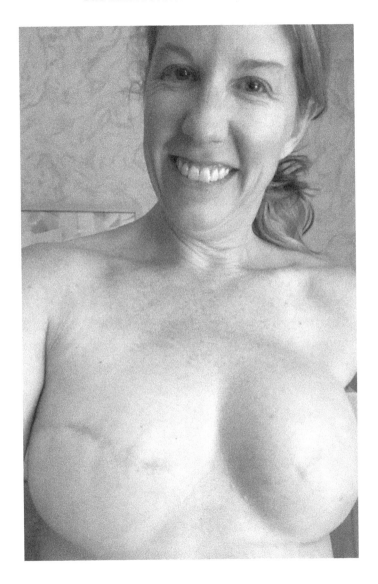

Plan B

The tattoo parlor was forty-five minutes outside the city, in an unassuming strip mall off a small highway. I sat in the parking lot and looked around. The tattoo parlor was sandwiched between ordinary businesses and places to run daily errands. Waiting in my car felt anticlimactic and thrilling at the same time. I sat there deeply reflecting on the decision, choices, and windy roads that led me here.

My girlfriends were supposed to get this tattoo with me. Initially, we intended to bring martinis in sippy cups and share laughs, drinks, and memories of my boobs. But, unfortunately, the COVID-19 global pandemic squashed those plans to be together. Alas, life was about plan B. I started this journey on my own, so it was fitting that this was how it would end. I had to walk the final steps on my own.

The Mastectomy I Always Wanted

The Path to Freedom

The tattoo artist was everything I had expected and more: curt, direct, and brilliant. And I respected him for this passion. He was an artist in his own right, fully committed to his work.

The first touch of the needle was more painful than I expected, which took me off guard. Then I took it as a good sign. It meant I finally had feeling in my breasts—another promise from the plastic surgeon that came true. I never thought I would have a sensation there again, forever doomed to bump into things I could not feel with my breasts. My implants felt foreign, like a necklace I could never take off after a long day.

Until now.

I felt the sting of the needles and the pressure of his hands at work. I was fully present in the pain, which was both exhilarating and challenging. I felt supported from afar by my husband, who was taking care of the kids; my friends, who sent me into battle with a meaningful necklace; and by the thousands of people who sent prayers for my strength over the journey. I was crossing the finish line alone but with an army of support behind me. I felt love and intention from guardian angels cheering me on from Heaven: *You got this. You did this. You are free.*

The Mastectomy I Always Wanted

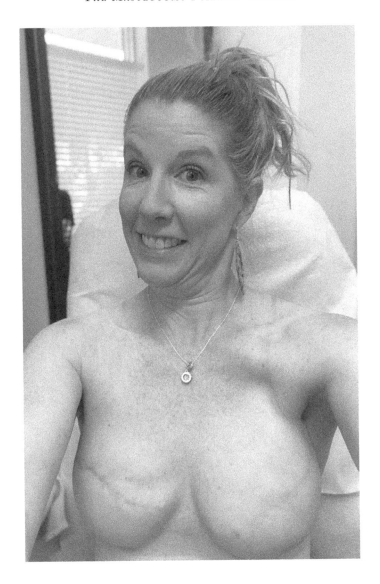

Erica Neubert Campbell

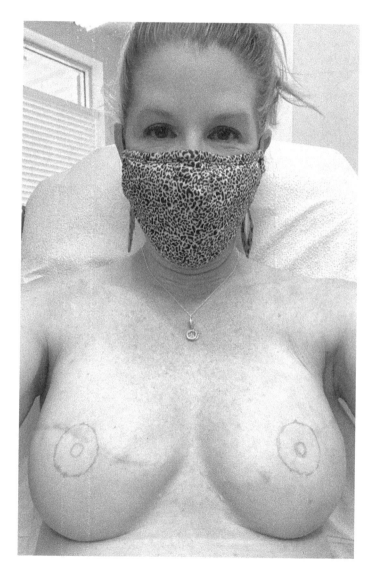

The Mastectomy I Always Wanted

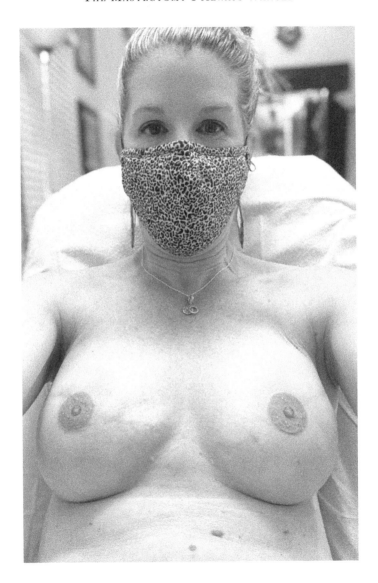

NINE

THE FINISH LINE

You're so hard on yourself. Take a moment. Sit back. Marvel at your life: at the grief that softened you, at the heartache that wisened you, at the suffering that strengthened you. Despite everything, you still grow. Be proud of this.

— Unknown

You Got This

Today, I marvel at my breasts. They are mine. They are not fake. They are the real miracles of mindset, modern medicine, and moving mountains. I still have lingering scars, and I like it that way. It reminds me that I am strong, resilient, and perfectly imperfect.

A double mastectomy is not something I would wish on my worst enemy—yet it was the gift I gave myself. The journey wasn't straightforward in the beginning. I started in a place of darkness and ended up in the light. This was the mastectomy I always wanted.

Today, I live cancer-free and without fear.

I am healed.

I no longer worry about breast cancer. Fear is no longer my captor. I dipped into vulnerability and witnessed my resilience. I trusted the process. I created a life that no one predicted or planned. It never made sense until now.

It's my honor to share this with you and loved ones you may know who are facing a similar journey. You got this, and I got you.

Top Ten Tips to Prepare for a Mastectomy

Tip 1: Take a Selfie of Your Breasts

I don't care if you think this is awkward or inappropriate. *Do this before your surgery.* You can take photos by yourself, with a friend, or even hire a professional photographer. Ensure you capture your original breasts from several angles. You will want to remember them and may have questions throughout the reconstruction process. Be brave and vulnerable. Give yourself space and time to say goodbye to this significant part of your body and history. I admired my breasts and expressed gratitude for their benefits over the years.

Tip 2: Designate a Lead Communicator

Whether you use emails, texts, CaringBridge, or carrier pigeon, appoint a friend or family member to handle your communications. Friends and family will have questions and a natural curiosity. They sincerely want to be helpful. However, the frequency of communications and the range of other people's emotions can be overwhelming. Plan to outsource information and updates. If people email or text you directly, set the expectation in advance that you might not reply. Let them know it's not personal or avoidance;

it's overwhelming. This will relieve the guilt you may feel and provide clarity for your supporters. It's a win-win for everyone.

Tip 3: Buy Cheap Clothes That Button or Zip Up in the Front

Get a small wardrobe of tops you can wear now, then dispose of them when you regain upper body mobility. Of course, you can use your existing clothes or buy expensive tops, but I wouldn't make a significant investment. These clothes are for a specific season of your life. Buy cheap, wear often, then let go. Don't waste your money or your mental energy. The time will come when you are ready to burn or donate those clothes.

Tip 4: Write in a Journal

Seriously. Even the toughest of women need to write. Your unconscious brain is holding on to emotions and feelings, which may be deeper than you realize. The mind is processing so much new information, and journaling helps create filters to sort out the most essential next steps. Journaling will allow your brain to relax and sleep better, too.

Invest in a paper journal and write at least once a day for weeks before and after your surgery. If you don't know what to write about, use journaling prompts. For example, write about five things you are grateful for, five things you are afraid of, five emotions you are feeling, and five things you are learning.

There is scientific evidence that using your hand to write on paper unlocks unconscious thoughts and begins to release them. Writing gives your mind a way to acknowledge your circumstances and how you feel about them. You need to express emotions for them to pass. Give your brain a break from processing alone. Journaling will help you let go.

Tip 5: Invest in Helpful Tools

Prepare yourself for sleep and showers. Get some plastic lanyard string to support you in showering with the drainage tubes once you get clearance from your doctor. This waterproof string can be reused and tied in a knot around the drainage bulbs so you can forget about them and enjoy your well-deserved shower.

Consider buying or renting an oversized recliner chair. Getting in and out of bed is hard, and a recliner can give you comfort and ease. In addition, invest in pillows that work for you. I suggest a wedge-shaped pillow to keep you slightly upright for sleeping. Sleep will accelerate the healing, and showers will bring you inexplicable joy.

Tip 6: Sign Up for Physical Therapy

You will want someone else to support you in massaging the scars, releasing the muscle tension, and building your confidence to return to full mobility. And you *will* regain full mobility. Do you hear me? I could not raise my hand above my shoulders due to pain and fear. Now I can do handstands. I encourage you to get a professional physical therapist to support you in this journey, stretch your limits, and safely build strength. You will need this even if you don't intend to do heavy lifting or handstands.

Tip 7: Sign Up for Mental Health Therapy

I resisted mental health counseling at first. I believed I was strong-willed, resilient, and well-balanced. But I listened to the advice of my surgeon and fellow cancer warriors to get past any stigmas. They convinced me that therapy was essential to healing and an investment in my overall health. My mind needed strengthening as much as my body. Despite feeling uneasy and filled with dread, I longed for a haven where I could speak my truth without judgment. I needed to find a safe space to be vulnerable and authentic. Although progress felt granular and slow, I gradually discovered an immense sense of grace, acceptance, and freedom. The time to talk allowed me to heal and grow in ways I never thought possible.

It's like renovating a house—you need a licensed professional to rebuild properly. To move forward, you must talk about your feelings and fears. There is no shame in asking for help, and there is no risk in trying. I promise this will help. Ask your doctor for a referral and sign up, even if it's only for a few sessions.

Tip 8: Take Naps during Your Recovery

Make no mistake: sleep is a challenge after surgery. I struggled for months and fought hard to create strategies to rest as much as possible. You will quickly look "back to normal" to the rest of the world, and life moves at lightning speed. Don't get upset if others overlook your discomfort and pain. They may forget, but you will not.

I invite you to rest up and take naps frequently. Request the space to heal at your own pace. Give yourself time. Patience and grace for myself and others became a powerful mantra while I recovered. The journey can feel long and lonely. Physical and mental breaks are necessary. If you pause and step back from responsibilities, you will return to your everyday life stronger.

Tip 9: Trust the Process

Many times, my plastic surgeon asked me to trust the process. I found this challenging in the beginning. I met many new medical professionals, and relationships initially felt rushed. I questioned whether a male doctor would understand the significance of a woman losing her breasts. Despite this hesitation, my doctor's excellent bedside manner gave me confidence. The speed of decision-making required a combination of research and gut instinct. Trust yourself. Once you pick your care team, believe they have your best interests at heart and let them do their job.

Also, trust yourself. If you do not believe in one of your doctors, find a replacement. Keep refining and trusting in your instincts. We are all in this together, and confidence is a massive part of the journey. Find out what trust means to you, write about it, and share it with your family, friends, and care team.

Tip 10: Have a Badass Attitude

No matter how confident or fearful you may be, know that you are infinitely tougher than you can imagine. Make your attitude the anchor that grounds you and keeps you strong. Many people will say, "I don't know how you got through a mastectomy." Your response will vary, but it will include baby steps and having no choice but to rise to the challenge. Make resilience your full-time job. You will become a professional badass. Find her inside you. She's ready to tackle any obstacles. Go for it.

And while you're at it, write to me with your badass story. Find me at **www.EricaNeubertCampbell.com** and submit your story.

Acknowledgments

To my incredibly supportive husband, Ian, who loves me unconditionally and creates big adventures together. You feed my body and soul. I am the luckiest woman in the world.

To my daughter, Amelia, who teaches me courage, forgiveness, and how to "glow up." I love you to the moon and back.

To my son, Duncan, who teaches me to trust, play, and bring a vision to life. You are my missing piece and Squishy Turkey.

To my dad, the biggest cheerleader in my life. To my wider family, including Scott, Kari, Greta, Bode, Gus, Robert, JoAnn, Keith, Katie, Ava, Alexa, and Ashton. To Patty and Cathy and the entire Nafz family, Karl and Melissa and the Werenskjold families, the Neubert family, the Pezanowski family, and more.

To friends that have become family, including Jane and Anita, the R Street Adventure Club of Lynne, Alli, Lissa, Amy, Claire, Eric, Mike, Jeff, Liz, Ken, and Becca, my Kappa Kappa Gamma family of Holly, Gabriella, and

Kate, and my Arlington Girls of Missy, Lisa, Holly, Claire, and Alison.

To my breast plastic surgeon, Dr. Jason Buseman, for building trust and walking this journey beside me with your technical brilliance and compassionate friendship. I am deeply grateful for the nursing team, surgeons, physical therapists, and mental health professionals at Methodist Hospital, Park Nicollet, and the Frauenshuh Cancer Center in St. Louis Park, MN. It takes a village.

To my teams, coaches, and mentors at Next Level Trainings, who encouraged me to get out of my comfort zone and transform my life. Special thanks to the B11 and LIT8 teams. You held up the mirror and inspired me to be the uncontested author of my life. Because of you, I am a powerful, authentic, loving woman.

To the women and men who supported me in reviewing, editing, and encouraging this book, including Kate, Erin, Andrea, Christine, Tim, Branwyn, Laura, Amy, Karen, Adam, the ladies of my 5 AM book club, and every woman I've met who has faced breast cancer.

I am forever grateful to Dara Beevas and the team at Wise Ink for their professional guidance and personal wisdom.

To the kids, families, and teams at Pinky Swear Foundation and Special Love. Thank you for allowing me to lead with head and heart. This work is my life purpose.

To my hero, Angelina Jolie, for publicly sharing your mastectomy journey in a *New York Times* Op-Ed in 2003. Your courage saved my life and thousands of other women.

To Taylor Swift for showing me what it looks like to use your voice and speak your truth. You moved me to be "Fearless," "Begin Again," and pull on the "Invisible String" of life.

To Katie Couric for inspiring me to advocate for preventative care and put myself on the line for other women and caregivers.

To all the incredible and generous supporters who brought this book to life.

In Honor Of:

Alissa Younkin
All the Breast Badasses
Aviva Walls
Claire Dempsey Wellinghoff
EZ
Hiro Sugimura
Irene Qualley Jaros & all her children
Kelli Nies & Cathy Puskar
Michelle Bresch
Michelle Grinsel
Mom & Grammy
Odessa Kees
Patty Nafz
Strong women & good friends

In Gratitude Of:

Alli Phillips
Amy & Jack Fiterman
Anonymous
Ashbaugh, McGee & Quinn Families
Brian & Hilary Mann
Bridget Handke
Campbell Family
Cathy Nafz
Claire & Matt King
Claire Andrews
Coach Party Hearty Marti
Cole Family
Dana Podgurski
Debbie Tam
DeCesare Family
Dodelin Family
Doyle Family
Dupuis Family
Edwin Parcher
Elaine R. Sugimura
Erik Dominguez
Erlanger Family
Friedlander Family
Gabriella & Chris Crane
Hanson Family
Imelda Brehmer
Jan Bresch

Jay & Laura Higgins
Jed Carlson
Jeff & Leigh Reid
JoAnn & Robert Campbell
John Coombs IV
Joy Biscornet Borek &
  Matt Borek
Karen Liu
Kate & Keith Mercier
Kate Simek
Kathy Russell
Kirby Family
Lapham Family
Lauren Greene
Liz Anderson
MacLachlan Family
Mark Family
Meehan Family
Mitch Marczewski Jr.
Murphy Family
Nettie Sparkman
Nikki Feinsot
Romy Parzick & Family
Royal Jaros
Sara & Corey Hoff
Sean Muir
Seem Family

Shah-Daly Family
Sloan Family
Stacia Stribling
Tammara Jenkins
Terri & Bill Tomoff
Troy Family
Tyson Family
Werenskjold Family
Wise Ink Team
Wong Family

ERICA NEUBERT CAMPBELL is a breast cancer survivor and a "cancer orphan" after losing her mother to breast cancer over twenty years ago. Since 1997, she has dedicated her life to supporting cancer patients and supporters. Erica currently leads the Pinky Swear Foundation, a nonprofit that keeps the promise to help kids with cancer and their families with financial and emotional support. She also volunteered for many years as a board member with Special Love, Inc., and counselor for Camp Fantastic, a summer sleepaway camp for children with cancer. You can learn more about these impactful organizations at **www.SpecialLove.org** and **www.PinkySwear.org**.

Her story is included in the book *Perspectives on Cancer: Cancer Patients, Survivors & Supporters Share Their Stories* released in 2023 and can be found on Amazon.com. She is also a contributing author to the magazine *Character Core* and has written articles on resilience, enthusiasm, and compassion.

She lives in Minneapolis, MN, with her loving husband, Ian, and children, Amelia and Duncan. You can find her traveling in a 2008 Winnebago RV in the summer, embracing the cold in the winter, and cheering enthusiastically on the sidelines of kid sports year-round. Erica loves authenticity, connection, and the unexpected ways a vision comes to life.

> Share your story, connect, and learn more at **www.EricaNeubertCampbell.com**.